Seriously Good!
GLUTEN-FREE COOKING

Seriously Good!
GLUTEN-FREE COOKING

PHIL VICKERY

PHOTOGRAPHY BY STEVE LEE

Kyle Books

This revised edition published in Great Britain in 2016 by
Kyle Books, an imprint of Kyle Cathie Ltd.
192-198 Vauxhall Bridge Road
London, SW1V 1DX
general.enquiries@kylebooks.com
www.kylebooks.com

First published in Great Britain in 2009 by Kyle Books

10 9 8 7 6 5 4 3 2 1

ISBN 978 0 85783 315 0

Text © 2009 by Phil Vickery, except for pages 42, 57, 77, 80, 91, 92, 114, 119, 128 and 155 © 2016 by Phil Vickery
Design © 2009 by Kyle Books
Photographs © 2009 by Steve Lee

Project Editor Danielle Di Michiel
Designed by Sarah Rock
Photography by Steve Lee
Home economy by Clare Greenstreet and Julia Alger
Prop styling by Liz Belton
Production by Sha Huxtable

Phil Vickery is hereby identified as the author of this work in accordance with Section 77 of the Copyright, Designs and Patents Act 1988.

A Cataloguing in Publication record for this title is available from the British Library.

Colour reproduction by Chromographics.
Printed and bound in China by C&C Offset Printing Co., Ltd.

Cook's notes

Using a fan oven
If you are using a fan oven, please refer to the manufacturer's handbook for the correct oven temperature conversion.

Raw eggs
Eating raw eggs, or eggs with runny yolks, or any food containing these, can cause food poisoning especially for anyone who is very young (babies to toddlers), elderly, pregnant or already unwell.

Strong stock
Where strong stock is listed in the ingredients, make the stock up using half the amount of water specified on the pack instructions.

Xanthan gum
Xanthan gum is a very useful dry ingredient that, when added to gluten-free flours, provides some of the elastic texture and quality that it would otherwise lack. It makes all the difference to gluten-free bread and should be available from most health food stores and major supermarket retailers.

Contents

INTRODUCTION

About ten years ago I started to make Christmas puddings and sell them at a Christmas fayre. The puddings were of very high quality, made with exceptional ingredients and attracted a good deal of attention. Business was brisk and the interest was infectious.

However after a while a trend began to emerge. A lot of people would approach us, look at our wares and stop to chat. But when offered a taste of the puddings they would decline, almost recoiling with horror as they explained: 'No, I can't – I'm coeliac; do you know what that means?' I would politely reply that I did know, having spent many years cooking in restaurants and hotels, adding that, in fact, the puddings were gluten-free! Their reaction was classic – like that of someone who's broken down in a storm in the middle of the night and the AA man turns up! They would then snap up three or four puddings apiece and tell their friends all about them – it was amazing.

I approached Coeliac UK, not only to learn a little more about the condition, but also to explore the idea of getting a Gluten-free logo on my puddings. My meetings with them over the weeks and months that followed were an eye-opener. The huge impact of this disease on sufferers is really quite scary.

Most chefs have little idea of what exactly coeliac disease is, much less what it involves – something that I believe needs to change. So with this in mind, and having carried out a great deal of research, I decided to write a book on the subject, which, unlike many others on the market, would be from a chef's point of view.

And here is the result! Covering all areas of cooking from bakes and stews to puds, and from breakfasts to pastry, the book has something for everyone.

Phil Vickery

Nov 15

WHAT IS COELIAC DISEASE?

Coeliac disease is frequently and widely misunderstood. It is often regarded as an allergy or simple food intolerance when it is in fact a lifelong, autoimmune disease affecting the gut and other parts of the body. It is caused by an inflammatory response to gluten, a protein found in wheat, barley and rye. Some people are also affected by oats. Gluten is a collective name for the type of protein found in these cereals. It is what gives bread its elasticity and cakes their spring and, unfortunately, even the tiniest amount of gluten can cause problems for people with coeliac disease.

Coeliac sufferers are sensitive to the presence of this protein in the digestive system. The small intestine is lined with small, finger-like projections called villi. These play a crucial role in digestion as they increase the surface area of the small intestine and allow essential nutrients to be absorbed into the bloodstream. However, for people with coeliac disease, when gluten comes into contact with the villi, it triggers a response by the immune system which attacks the villi, as if it were a 'foreign' substance. The villi very quickly become damaged and inflamed and incapable of extracting key nutrients from the food we eat. This results in a range of different problems with varying severity.

WHAT ARE THE SYMPTOMS?

The variety of gastrointestinal symptoms that may be present in patients with coeliac disease is great as the malabsorption described above quickly leads to cramps, gas, bloating, flatulence and diarrhoea. It is quite common for these to be put down to irritable bowel syndrome (IBS), and only later to be recognised as coeliac disease.

Diarrhoea is certainly common and yet it is important to note that sufferers can present many and varied symptoms; some may have a normal bowel habit or even tend towards constipation, children may not gain weight or grow properly, while adults may find they lose weight. Malabsorption may also leave people tired and weak, because of anaemia caused by iron or folate deficiency.

In fact, rather than experiencing bowel problems, many coeliac sufferers approach their doctor because of extreme tiredness (due to chronic poor iron absorption) and psychological problems such as depression. There can also be a calcium deficiency due to malabsorption, resulting in low bone density and sometimes even fractures (as a result of osteoporosis). Bone and muscle pain can also be a problem. Ulcers in the mouth or a blistering, itchy skin rash mostly on the elbows and knees (called dermatitis herpetiformis) are also symptoms of coeliac disaese.

HOW DO I GET DIAGNOSED?

Firstly, if you suspect you may suffer from coeliac disease, don't panic. Just remember, it is entirely manageable with a controlled diet. In fact, if you are one of the many, many undiagnosed sufferers, you'll probably be pleased to find out that you really do have a condition and, better yet, that there is a course of action to alleviate the symptoms.

There is a clear procedure for diagnosing coeliac disease. The first thing to do is talk through your symptoms with your GP as

TYPICAL SYMPTOMS

Diarrhoea, fatigue and iron deficiency stem directly from the malabsorption of nutrients, but there is a range of other symptoms, including:

- Bloating
- Abdominal pains
- Nausea
- Weight loss (but not in all cases)
- Mouth ulcers
- Hair loss
- Skin rash
- Defective tooth enamel

they will be able to perform a simple coeliac screening blood test in order to detect disease-specific antibodies. It is important to follow your normal diet leading up to the test as confirmation is provided by the presence of antibodies in the blood which have been triggered by a coeliac's response to gluten. It is quite common for people to go undiagnosed, as if they have followed a gluten-free diet for a number of days, the immune system has already slowed down antibody production to 'normal' levels and the tests therefore prove a false negative. To obtain an accurate test result it is necessary to consume food that contains gluten every day for a minimum of six weeks before blood is taken for the test.

If the test proves positive, it is recommended that people then have an intestinal biopsy, which examines the appearance of the villi in the small intestine under a microscope to check for damage. This will provide you with confirmation of your diagnosis before you embark on a lifelong diet of gluten avoidance. The small intestinal biopsy must also be done after a gluten-based diet for accurate diagnosis as a biopsy specimen taken on a gluten-free diet might show a completely normal intestinal lining. However, children may not always need a biopsy when being tested as if they have symptoms of coeliac disease and a blood test that shows high levels of antibodies, a second antibody blood test followed by a genetic test can be used to confirm the diagnosis.

These new guidelines reflect the improved accuracy and reliability of the antibody blood tests. The waiting time for biopsy may be several weeks and can be a factor in delaying diagnosis and starting treatment with the gluten-free diet. If there is no need for biopsy, the diagnosis process is much quicker, which is good news for the child.

WHAT IS THE TREATMENT?

The complete treatment for coeliac disease is a gluten-free diet and this means that wheat, barley, rye and their derivatives must all be avoided. The most obvious sources of gluten in the diet are pastas, cereals, breads, flours, pizza bases, pastry, cakes and biscuits. Most people are able to tolerate uncontaminated oats without a problem, although some people with coeliac disease may be sensitive and will need to avoid them.

Strict adherence to the diet allows the intestines to heal, leading to resolution of symptoms and reducing the risk of complications like osteoporosis.

WHAT CAN I EAT?

There is plenty of food that is naturally gluten-free and should be included in your diet. In particular, carbohydrate-rich foods such as potatoes, rice and maize do not contain gluten. And similarly, all fresh meat, poultry and fish, all fresh fruit and vegetables, fresh herbs, individual spices, dried pulses, rice noodles, potatoes, plain nuts, eggs, dairy products, sugar, honey, pure oils and vinegars, vanilla extract and fresh yeast. In fact, the coeliac diet has the potential to be one of the healthiest around because of the increased emphasis placed upon eating fresh, natural and unadulterated food. Furthermore, if gluten in the digestive system has been hampering the absorption of adequate vitamins and minerals into the bloodstream, then a coeliac diet should soon restore them to healthy levels and lead to a much enhanced feeling of overall wellbeing.

In addition, more and more manufacturers are producing gluten-free substitute foods, such as gluten-free bread, crackers and pasta, some of which are almost indistinguishable from their gluten-containing counterparts. Rice noodles are a good staple for the store cupboard, as are rice paper wrappers, which are great for 'wraps' in place of flour tortillas. Poppadums are usually made from lentil flour and often don't contain gluten and instead of wheat-based soy sauce, look out for Japanese tamari soy sauce, which is made from soya beans and rice rather than wheat flour. Coeliac UK, the leading charity for people with coeliac disease, has a useful Gluten-free Checklist which can be accessed at www.coeliac.org.uk/GlutenFreeChecklist so you can check what is and isn't suitable for your gluten-free diet.The Charity also produces information on thousands of products you can eat on a gluten-free diet which is available in a range of formats including on their mobile phone app, online and in printed form.

FOOD LABELS

You can tell from a food label whether or not a product is suitable for a gluten-free diet as allergen labelling legislation means that manufacturers have to list all the ingredients in food products. In addition, allergens, including gluten-containing cereals, must be emphasised in the ingredients, for example in bold lettering. When shopping and cooking, always check the label to make sure you choose a suitable product and pay special attention to the list of less-obvious foods and drinks that may include gluten without you realising it (see right).

FOODS THAT ARE NATURALLY GLUTEN-FREE

- all fresh meat and fish
- all fresh fruit and vegetables
- fresh herbs and individual spices
- corn and cornmeal (maize/sweetcorn)
- dried peas, lentils, pulses and beans
- rice and wild rice
- rice bran
- rice noodles
- plain nuts and seeds
- eggs
- dairy products – milk, cream, natural yogurt, cheese
- soya and plain tofu
- sugar
- honey
- golden syrup
- maple syrup
- treacle
- jams and marmalade
- pure oils and fats
- vinegars
- tomato purée
- vanilla essence and extract
- fresh yeast

FOODS AND DRINKS THAT MAY INCLUDE GLUTEN WITHOUT YOU REALISING IT

- baking powder
- communion wafers
- 'corn tortillas' may also contain regular flour
- frozen chips – these may be coated with flour
- stock cubes/powder
- vegetable soup may contain pearl barley
- seasoning mixes
- mustard products
- packet suet may have flour in it to stop it sticking together
- commercial salad dressings and mayonnaise
- soy sauce (there are gluten-free brands available)
- dry-roasted nuts
- pretzels
- Bombay mix
- Scotch eggs
- food that has been deep-fried with other gluten-containing food, e.g. battered fish and chips
- flavoured crisps
- malted milk drinks
- barley water or flavoured barley water
- beer, lager, stout and ale

GLUTEN-FREE ALTERNATIVES

In general, it is a good idea to be wary of cereals if you are following a gluten-free diet and yet there are a number of naturally gluten-free varieties that are worth knowing about as they give a similar result to cooking with regular flour and cereals and will enable you to try recipes that are otherwise out of bounds. As with all other foods, it is best to approach with a degree of caution so check the labelling. Alternative gluten-free grains include:

- rice flour
- tapioca flour/cassava flour
- potato flour
- cornflour
- ground cornmeal (polenta)
- soya flour
- gram flour/chickpea flour
- chestnut flour
- buckwheat flour
- lotus root flour
- carob flour
- millet flour
- quinoa flour
- sorghum
- arrowroot
- linseed
- sago
- teff

WHAT ABOUT CONTAMINATION?

Dry, gluten-containing ingredients like flour and breadcrumbs are high-risk ingredients for contamination and cross-contamination when you are producing gluten-free meals, and so it is a good idea to implement an organised system of separation in the kitchen. Steps to avoid contamination include:

- cleaning surfaces immediately before their use

- using clean frying oil for chips and gluten-free foods – do NOT reuse oil that has cooked breaded or battered products

- keeping all pans, utensils and colanders separate during preparation and cooking

- using a clean grill, separate toaster or toaster bags to make gluten-free toast

- making sure that butter or spreads are not contaminated with breadcrumbs

- using squeezy bottles to help avoid contamination through the dipping of spoons or knives

THIS BOOK

When you are gluten-free there is no reason why you can't enjoy really delicious, flavourful food. In fact, a gluten-free diet not only offers the chance to improve the quality of the food you eat by cooking with fresh, unadulterated ingredients but also to stretch your tastebuds with new ideas and flavour combinations. The recipes in this book are all about opening out the gluten-free diet – giving you food to enjoy, food that is nutritious and food that will make you feel seriously good!

COELIAC UK

Coeliac UK is the leading charity working for people with coeliac disease and dermatitis herpetiformis (DH).

Their mission is to improve the lives of people living with the condition through information, support, campaigning and research. Their vision is that the needs of people with coeliac disease and DH are universally recognised and met.

Coeliac UK offers a range of support services, providing expert and independent information to help people with coeliac disease manage their health and diet.

They produce a comprehensive range of information booklets, leaflets and publications. The Helpline and the website, featuring a special Members Only Area, provide additional news, information and advice.

They also have a smartphone app, Gluten-free on the Move, to help you shop for gluten-free items, and it even includes a handy scanner so you can scan items as you shop.

Members are a vital part of Coeliac UK's work as campaigners, fundraisers and volunteers. There are many ways people can get involved with Coeliac UK, including helping to raise awareness and improve life for people who are living life gluten-free.

If you are diagnosed with coeliac disease or dermatitis herpetiformis and would like to become a Member of Coeliac UK, or if you think that you or a family member may have coeliac disease, please call 0333 332 2033 or visit their website at www.coeliac.org.uk.

BREAKFASTS, SMOOTHIES & DRINKS

THE RECIPES: PINK GRAPEFRUIT 'GET-ME-UP' / CARROT, GINGER, CELERY, BEETROOT AND APPLE JUICE / BLUEBERRY MUSH WITH HONEYCOMB AND YOGURT / SPICED APPLE COMPOTE WITH THICK YOGURT / QUICK CRAB AND MUSHROOM KEDGEREE WITH PARSLEY BUTTER / SALT AND PEPPER EGGS ON RICE WAFFLES / TWICE COOKED FLAT MUSHROOMS WITH BASIL PANCAKES / BREAKFAST FRUIT SEED BARS / CHILLED TOMATO AND TARRAGON WATER / ICED GINGER TEA / FRESH BASIL CORDIAL / MELON AND CUCUMBER YOGURT SMOOTHIE / FROZEN CAPPUCCINOS / FRESH BLACKBERRY CORDIAL / FRESH SWEET AND SOUR MINT LEMONADE

PINK GRAPEFRUIT
'GET-ME-UP'

This is a nice drink for breakfast. Pink grapefruits were all the rage in the late 70s but they seem to have gone off the radar slightly. I like them in drinks, mousses (see the Light Pink Grapefruit Mousse recipe on page 186) and salads and with rich meats such as goose or duck.

juice of 4 ruby red pink grapefruit
juice of 4 limes
6 tablespoons clear honey
5 sprigs fresh mint

Place the grapefruit and lime juices in a glass jug and add enough clear honey to taste. It may take a bit of time to mix everything together, but keep stirring. Finally, bruise the mint leaves with the back of a knife and stir into the juice. Pour into glasses to serve.

CARROT, GINGER, CELERY, BEETROOT AND APPLE JUICE

This is Fern's favourite breakfast drink – she loves it! It has a bit of a kick and such a beautiful colour and flavour.

2 large organic carrots, peeled
100g fresh ginger, peeled
4 celery sticks
4 medium beetroot, cooked

4 large, sweet, British eating apples, e.g. Cox's, Orange Pippin or Russet
pinch of dried chilli flakes

Blitz all the ingredients together in a juicer. Chill in the fridge. Serve the very well chilled juice in small glasses.

If you don't have a juicer, place all the ingredients in a food processor or blender and whizz to make a purée. Pour into a sieve set over a large jug to remove any bits.

BLUEBERRY MUSH WITH HONEYCOMB AND YOGURT

SERVES: 4
PREPARATION: 10mins
COOKING: 15mins

This is a great way for adults and kids to eat extra fruit and seeds. It's a delicious way to kick-start the day – try it at the weekend when you've got a bit more time!

50g sesame seeds

75g sunflower seeds

50g pine nuts

50g walnuts

50g cashews

2 tablespoons extra virgin olive oil

2 ripe bananas

100g fresh blueberries

juice of 2 limes

75g semi-dried blueberries

500g thick natural Greek yogurt

50g honeycomb, chopped into small pieces

50g clear honey

100g gluten-free sweet puffed rice cereal

Preheat the oven to 200°C/400°F/gas mark 6. Place the seeds and nuts on a baking tray, drizzle the oil over, then cook for 1–2 minutes or until lightly toasted and browned. Set aside to cool.

Meanwhile, place the bananas and half the fresh blueberries in a bowl and add the lime juice. Gently break down the fruit with a fork, then add the semi-dried blueberries. Stir in the yogurt, honeycomb and honey and mix well.

Stir in the cooked seeds, half the puffed rice and the rest of the fresh blueberries. Set aside for 10 minutes, then stir again and divide between 4 bowls.

Sprinkle with the remaining puffed rice and serve.

SERVES: 4
PREPARATION: 35mins
COOKING: 30mins

SPICED APPLE COMPOTE WITH THICK YOGURT

I'm a real lover of Bramley apples; my mum would stew them and then serve them with a large jug of custard - delicious! But they also make a great breakfast pick-me-up: sharp, packed full of flavour and very good for you. What else do you need in the morning?

4 large Bramley apples, peeled and cored

150g caster sugar

1 teaspoon ground cinnamon

finely grated zest and juice of 1 lemon

finely grated zest and juice of 1 orange

pinch or two of citric acid powder (optional)

85g sunflower seeds

1 teaspoon olive oil

250g thick Greek yogurt

clear honey or chopped honeycomb and freshly
    grated nutmeg, to serve

Place the apples, sugar, cinnamon, lemon and orange zest and juice in a saucepan. Bring to the boil, then reduce the temperature and simmer gently for 10–12 minutes until you have a thick apple stew.

Once cooked, the mixture should be slightly dry, not too wet and nice and thick. Cool the purée, then chill in the fridge.

For an extra kick of tartness you can add a pinch or two of citric acid powder, this really boosts the deep apple flavour of the Bramleys. Be careful though - too much and the purée will develop a metallic taste.

Lightly fry the sunflower seeds in the olive oil, until just browned and slightly crunchy, then cool.

Spoon the chilled purée into individual glass bowls, then top with a large blob of yogurt. Sprinkle with a few seeds, a little drizzle of clear honey or some chopped honeycomb and a light dusting of fresh nutmeg, to serve.

QUICK CRAB AND MUSHROOM KEDGEREE

SERVES: 2–4
PREPARATION: 10mins
COOKING: 15mins

Kedgeree is a marvellous dish and a great old English favourite. This is a twist on the classic recipe - simple and so tasty.

3 x 200g sachets microwaveable plain boiled rice
115g butter
225g baby button mushrooms, halved
4 spring onions, chopped
450g fresh white crab meat
4 tablespoons roughly chopped fresh parsley
2 tablespoons vegetable oil
1 egg, beaten
salt and freshly ground black pepper

Warm the rice in the microwave on High for 2 minutes. Heat half the butter in a non-stick wok, then warm the rest in a separate pan. Add the mushrooms to the wok and cook for 2–3 minutes.

Add the spring onions, crab meat and parsley and cook for 2–3 minutes.

In a separate non-stick wok, heat the oil. Add the beaten egg and cook over a gentle heat, stirring constantly until the egg is scrambled.

Add the warmed rice to the crab mixture and mix well. Then add the egg to the rice, stir well and season.

Finally, stir in the remaining melted butter and serve.

SERVES: 4
PREPARATION: 5mins
COOKING: 15mins

SALT AND PEPPER EGGS ON RICE WAFFLES

This is a very simple recipe, but a really nice way to start the day. The classic combination of bacon and eggs with waffles is delicious.

For the waffles

oil, for greasing

2 large eggs

2 tablespoons vegetable oil

250ml milk

250g brown rice flour

pinch of salt

½ teaspoon gluten-free baking powder

½ teaspoon bicarbonate of soda

For the eggs

4 rashers streaky bacon, sliced into strips

1 teaspoon vinegar

4 large, very fresh eggs

cracked black pepper

sea salt

handful of fresh basil leaves, shredded

Oil and preheat the waffle maker. Using an electric whisk, blend the eggs, vegetable oil and milk together.

Combine the rice flour, salt, baking powder and bicarbonate of soda in a bowl. Gradually whisk the dry ingredients into the wet mixture until you have a smooth, thickish batter.

Pour one quarter of the batter into the base of the hot waffle iron and cook for about 3 minutes, depending on your waffle iron. When the waffles are done, place them in a warm oven, until you are ready to eat. Repeat with the remaining mixture.

If you don't have a waffle iron, use the batter to make four pancakes. Preheat a little oil in a large frying pan and spoon the batter into the pan to make four even-sized pancakes. Cook on one side until golden brown and then flip the pancakes to cook the other side.

Fry the bacon strips in a non-stick pan, until crispy. Next poach the eggs: add the vinegar to a pan of simmering water and carefully crack in the eggs. Poach for about 2 minutes, the yolks should still be soft.

Scoop the eggs out with a slotted spoon, and pop each one on top of a warm waffle. Season with cracked black pepper, a touch of salt on the egg (not too much, the bacon is salty too) and scatter over the crispy bacon and the basil.

FLAT MUSHROOMS WITH BASIL PANCAKES

SERVES: 4
PREPARATION: 15mins
COOKING: 25mins

When you grill mushrooms, they take on a different texture entirely, they become almost meat-like. If you combine that with twice cooking them, you really concentrate the flavours and textures further. You can serve these with a little grilled bacon or even a nice poached fillet of smoked haddock and a poached egg.

8 large flat mushrooms (the darker the better)

6 tablespoons olive oil

salt and freshly ground black pepper

For the pancakes

115g fine rice flour

½ teaspoon gluten-free baking powder

½ teaspoon cracked black pepper

1 medium egg

1½ tablespoons sunflower oil

284ml carton buttermilk

3 tablespoons finely chopped basil

3 tablespoons olive oil

55g unsalted butter, melted, to serve

Preheat the grill to the hottest setting. Trim the stalks off the mushrooms, so they are level with the gills. Place the olive oil in a large, ovenproof frying pan and heat.

Add the mushrooms gill-side down, season really well, wait until they sizzle and then place the whole pan under the grill. Cook for 10–15 minutes, or until soft. Once cooked, remove and cool in a colander, straining off all the juices.

Next make the pancakes: place the rice flour, baking powder, cracked black pepper and a pinch of salt in a bowl.

In a separate bowl, place the egg, sunflower oil and buttermilk and whisk well together. Gradually add the wet mix to the dry mix; you should end up with a loose but thickish batter. Finally, stir in the basil.

Heat a large non-stick frying pan and then add the olive oil. Spoon in enough pancake mixture to make 8 small pancakes. Cook for 2–3 minutes until light brown, then flip over and cook the other side. Repeat until all the mixture is cooked, place the cooked pancakes on a warm plate, covered in foil, to keep them hot.

Reheat the mushrooms under a hot grill; they will take on an almost meaty texture. Serve with the pancakes with a little melted butter.

BREAKFAST FRUIT SEED BARS

These bars are a winner with the kids at home. I think it's partly because of the texture – crunchy with a lovely background flavour, and of course the sweetness of the sugar. You can omit the sugar if you want, but the texture will be slightly crumblier.

100g sunflower seeds

100g sesame seeds

100g pumpkin seeds

100g semi-dried cranberries

100g semi-dried blueberries

100g gluten-free porridge oats

2 tablespoons soft brown sugar

1 teaspoon ground cumin seeds

1 teaspoon ground cinnamon

1 teaspoon ground coriander

1 x 397g tin condensed milk

150g unsalted butter, cut into small cubes

Preheat the oven to 180°C/350°F/gas mark 4. Line a 24cm square baking tin with baking parchment.

Place the seeds, fruit, oats, sugar and spices in a large bowl and mix well.

Put the condensed milk and butter into a bowl and place over a pan of gently simmering water. Melt together until well blended and hot. This will take about 15 minutes.

Stir the butter mixture into the fruit and seeds and mix really well.

Spoon the mixture into the tin and pack down lightly with the back of the spoon.

Bake for about 20 minutes, until slightly golden. Remove from the oven, cool and cut into bars.

CHILLED TOMATO AND TARRAGON WATER

This is an unusual way of using up over-ripe tomatoes; coupled with a little vinegar, sugar and fresh tarragon it makes a great summer aperitif.

10 large, very soft, over-ripe tomatoes

1 small bunch fresh tarragon

6 tablespoons sherry vinegar

2 tablespoons caster sugar

salt and ground white pepper

a few drops of Tabasco sauce

Simply place the tomatoes and tarragon in a food processor and blitz until puréed. Pour into a jelly bag, clean muslin or tea-towel laid into a 28cm colander, placed over a bowl large enough to catch the juice. The colander should not come into contact with the strained juice.

Leave the purée overnight in a fridge to drip through and produce a clear tomato water. Taste and adjust the flavour with vinegar, sugar, salt and pepper.

Serve, super chilled, in small glasses with a dash of Tabasco sauce.

SERVES: 4
PREPARATION: 5mins
COOKING: 10mins

ICED GINGER TEA

This lovely refreshing drink can be served either hot or chilled with ice cubes. I first came across this tea whilst staying with my dear friends Charles and Allan, but the recipe was actually first made by their housekeepers, Marie and Bernadette.

400g fresh ginger, finely chopped

1.25 litres boiling water

3-4 tablespoons sugar

ice cubes and lemon wedges, to serve

Place the chopped ginger in a teapot. Pour over the boiling water, add the sugar to taste and stir to dissolve. If serving hot, allow to infuse for 2 minutes and then pour into mugs. If serving cold, leave to cool completely. Serve in tall glasses with ice cubes and lemon wedges.

FRESH BASIL CORDIAL

MAKES: approx 1 litre
PREPARATION: 15mins
COOKING: 15mins

Quite an unusual cordial, but very refreshing, especially when served with plenty of ice cubes. I once had basil ice cream made by Joyce Molyneaux at her famous restaurant The Carved Angel in Dartmouth and thought that sweet basil works very well indeed. The citric acid (which can be purchased from chemists) really gives the drink a kick and cuts the sweetness.

600g caster sugar
600ml water
2 vanilla pods, split
2 tablespoons golden syrup
12 level teaspoons citric acid
2 large bunches fresh basil, roughly chopped
fresh basil leaves, ice cubes and soda water, to serve

Place the sugar, water, vanilla pods and golden syrup in a saucepan and bring to a simmer until the sugar has dissolved.

Add the citric acid, and dissolve, then add the basil and allow it to wilt slightly.

Remove from the heat, cover with clingfilm and leave to cool completely. Once cooled, strain through a sieve, then bottle and chill well.

To serve, pour 2cm basil syrup into tall tumblers, add 5–6 bruised fresh basil leaves and lots of ice. Top up with soda water and serve; your guests will be surprised, trust me! This syrup will keep in the fridge for a couple of weeks.

SERVES: 4
PREPARATION: 10mins
COOKING: none

MELON AND CUCUMBER YOGURT SMOOTHIE

Smoothies are now big business and it's easy to spend £3-4 on one when you're out and about, but they are so simple to make and literally take minutes to prepare. I like the cool flavour of melon and cucumber together. Use a perfumed melon such as galia, honeydew or charentais for a deeper-flavoured end result.

1 small ripe melon
1 cucumber, peeled and chopped
juice of 2 limes
6 fresh basil leaves
4 tablespoons Greek yogurt
1-2 tablespoons clear honey
good handful ice cubes

Cut the melon in half and scoop out the seeds. Using a spoon, scoop the flesh into a food processor or liquidiser. Add the cucumber and lime juice and blitz well.

Add the basil to the liquidiser with the yogurt, 1 tablespoon of the honey and the ice cubes.

Blend until smooth, then taste and add more honey if you think it needs it.

Pour into tall glasses and serve at once.

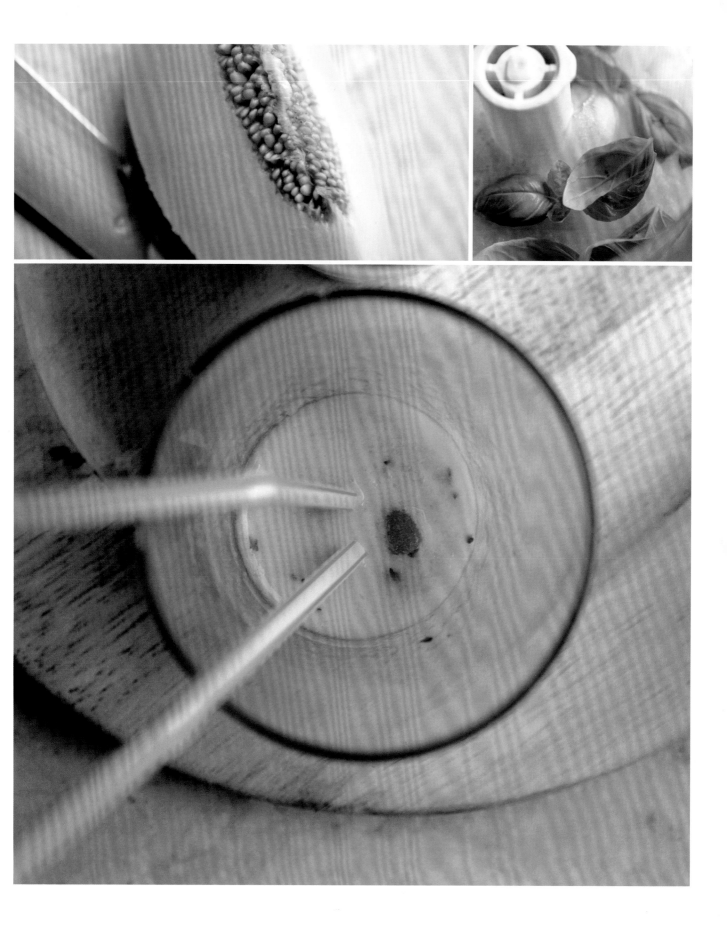

FROZEN CAPPUCCINOS

This is a nice treat to serve at the end of a meal, especially in the summer months. It's equally good as a light pudding, with a small ball of vanilla ice cream served separately.

12 ice cubes

100ml espresso or strong coffee, cooled for
   20 minutes

50ml coffee cream liqueur

300ml milk

4 teaspoons cocoa powder or gluten-free
   drinking chocolate, to serve

Blend the ice cubes, coffee, liqueur and milk in a liquidiser for 3 minutes. Pour into 4 tall glasses and sprinkle with cocoa powder or drinking chocolate, to serve.

MAKES: approx 800ml
PREPARATION: 20mins
plus 4 hours straining
COOKING: 40mins

FRESH BLACKBERRY CORDIAL

This recipe is a great way of using soft fruit just past its best. You can always freeze summer fruit and make the cordial later. In fact, I reckon certain fruits release more juice and colour when frozen and defrosted, for instance raspberries and blackcurrants. Citric acid adds an extra tang to the cordial.

When straining the juice, through a jelly bag or clean tea-towel, make sure that is not too perfumed from the washing powder (yes, it's true, it can really flavour jellies and syrups. The best thing is to use muslin, clean and simple).

3kg very ripe blackberries (the riper the better)
350ml water
juice of 2 large lemons

granulated sugar (see method for amount)
citric acid (optional, see method for amount)
ice, lime slices and soda or sparkling water, to serve

Pick over the fruit and remove any bits and pieces, including any wildlife! Wash carefully but thoroughly and drain well.

Place the water, lemon juice and fruit in a non-aluminium pan (aluminium reacts with the acid in the fruits) and warm gently.

Simmer gently for about 15-20 minutes, until all the beautiful juice and colour have been cooked from the fruit.

Strain the juice through a jelly bag, clean tea-towel or muslin. Leave for a minimum of 4 hours or until all the juice is through. Do not be tempted to push the fruit through as this will make the syrup cloudy.

Measure the amount of drained juice into a clean pan and for every 600ml juice, add 350g sugar and 1 teaspoon citric acid, if using.

Bring the juice to the boil, skim well and cook for about 20 minutes until slightly thickened, then cool and bottle. Chill well.

To serve, add a few ice cubes and some lime slices to a large glass, half fill with cordial and top up with soda or sparkling water. The cordial will keep for up to 2 weeks in the fridge.

FRESH SWEET AND SOUR MINT LEMONADE

MAKES: approx 2 litres
PREPARATION: 30mins plus overnight chilling
COOKING: none

Well, this is delicious, simple and easy to make. The citric acid really gives the lemonade a sharp edge, similar to the sour fruit drops you can buy. Remember, if the end result is too sweet, then add water to dilute it like a cordial. Soda or sparkling water works equally well.

3 large soft lemons
2 large soft limes
900g caster sugar
25g citric acid
6 tablespoons roughly chopped mint leaves and stalks

1 teaspoon salt
2 litres boiling water
6 tablespoons finely chopped mint leaves
crushed sea salt, ice cubes, lemon and lime wedges, to serve

Peel the lemons with a vegetable peeler, then squeeze out all the juice.

Do the same with the limes.

Place the sugar, juices, peel, citric acid, chopped mint leaves and stalks and salt in a large bowl, then stir well.

Pour over the boiling water, cover with clingfilm then leave to cool. Once cooled, chill in the fridge overnight.

Next day, strain through a fine sieve, then add the finely chopped mint leaves.

Dilute with a little water if it is too sweet.

Serve in tall tumblers, the tops frosted with a little crushed sea salt, similar to a margarita, with loads of ice cubes, lemon and lime wedges.

SNACKS & QUICK FOOD

THE RECIPES: ONION BHAJIS WITH MANGO AND MINT YOGURT / SMOKED SALMON AND BROAD BEAN SALAD / CRISPY PORK SALAD WITH LEMON DRESSING / STUFFED CELERY STICKS WITH PARMA HAM / MARINATED SMOKED SALMON WITH WHITE RADISH AND PICKLED GINGER / SAUTÉED PRAWNS WITH AVOCADO AND CORN SALSA / ROAST CHICKEN STOCK WITH FRESH PARSLEY AND LEMON / BASMATI RICE AND PARMESAN SPOON BREAD / JUICY CHICKEN BITES WITH GREEN HORSERADISH MAYO / POPCORN CHICKEN WITH SPICY DIPPING SAUCE / QUICK TOFU MISO SOUP / BORLOTTI BEAN, CHILLI AND PINE NUT BAKE / PASTA GRATIN WITH PEPPERS AND SMOKED GARLIC / FERN'S HONEYED BAKED BEANS ON MUSTARD DROP SCONES / STIR-FRIED RICE WITH AVOCADO AND HORSERADISH / SIMPLE TOMATO, PRAWN AND OUZO STEW / SAUTÉED CHICKEN LIVERS WITH TARRAGON MUFFINS / SEARED TUNA WITH EGG, CAPER AND HERB DRESSING

SERVES: 4
PREPARATION: 10mins
plus 1 hour marinating
COOKING: 6-8mins

ONION BHAJIS WITH MANGO AND MINT YOGURT

A great favourite on *Ready Steady Cook*, these taste as good as they look. Serve them as a tasty quick starter or as a main course with a little salad. We sometimes have these as a telly meal with the kids. You have to make the mixture and cook it straight away to get the best results and don't try and cook too quickly.

For the sauce
½ x 410g can sliced mangoes, well drained or
　½ medium ripe mango, peeled and stoned
225ml natural yogurt
2 tablespoons chopped fresh mint

For the bhajis
1 medium onion, halved and very thinly sliced
1 heaped teaspoon ground turmeric

1 teaspoon ground cumin
4 tablespoons chopped fresh coriander
225g chickpea (gram) flour
½ teaspoon gluten-free baking powder
approximately 250-300ml sparkling water
vegetable oil, for deep frying
salt and freshly ground black pepper
green salad, to serve

Place the mango and yogurt in a liquidiser and blitz until smooth. Spoon into a bowl, stir in the chopped mint, cover and leave to marinate for about 1 hour at room temperature.

Place the onion, spices, coriander, flour and baking powder in a large bowl and mix well. Add enough sparkling water to form a wet, soft mixture. The mixture should not be runny. Fill a 30cm deep frying pan or wok with 4cm of vegetable oil, then heat to 175°C or until a cube of bread browns in 15 seconds.

Pull off lumps of the mixture about the size of small walnuts. Drop no more than 4-5 lumps at a time into the hot oil. They will colour very quickly due to the turmeric. Once they have cooked for 3 minutes, flip over and cook the other side until nice and evenly browned. Drain well on kitchen paper, place the cooked bhajis on a warm plate, covered in foil, to keep them hot.

Let the oil come back to the right temperature and repeat the process until all the mixture is used up.

To serve, place on warm plates and drizzle over a little dressing and serve with a green salad.

SMOKED SALMON AND BROAD BEAN SALAD

SERVES: 4
PREPARATION: 15mins
COOKING: none

I love broad beans – they are so delicious. I like to use them all year round so I often use frozen beans. Simply plunge them into boiling salted water, bring them back to the boil and drain – they're really sweet and tasty. Couple them with smoked salmon and mustard dressing to make a nice easy snack.

2 tablespoons white wine vinegar

2 teaspoons gluten-free Dijon mustard

4 tablespoons sunflower oil

4 tablespoons extra virgin olive oil

250g frozen broad beans, cooked, refreshed and well drained

1 medium Cos lettuce, finely shredded

16 baby plum tomatoes, halved

16 small mozzarella balls, halved

225g smoked salmon slices, cut into strips

salt and freshly ground black pepper

Make the dressing by whisking the vinegar and mustard with a little salt and pepper.

Gradually add the oils until you have a thickish dressing, then taste and adjust the seasoning if needed.

Place the cooked beans, lettuce and plum tomatoes in a large bowl and mix well. Add three quarters of the dressing and mix well again.

Pile onto plates, then arrange the mozzarella around the edge of the salad.

Lay over the smoked salmon strips and spoon over the rest of the dressing.

SERVES: 4
PREPARATION: 15mins
COOKING: 10mins

CRISPY PORK SALAD WITH LEMON DRESSING

This salad makes a little great value-for-money British pork go a long way. It's a really simple, tasty salad that is quite unusual.

4 rashers streaky, dry-cured bacon, cut into strips

400g minced British pork

1 tablespoon Chinese five spice powder

2 tablespoons vegetable oil

salt and freshly ground black pepper

For the dressing

3 tablespoons clear honey

finely grated zest and juice of 2 large lemons

3 tablespoons olive oil

1 tablespoon molasses

2 tablespoons tamari

1 teaspoon caster sugar

For the salad

½ iceberg lettuce, very finely sliced

1 small mouli (Japanese radish), very finely sliced into shreds

8 pepperdew peppers, roughly chopped

1 small bunch of watercress

Preheat the oven to 200°C/400°F/gas mark 6. Heat a non-stick frying pan and cook the bacon strips until crispy. Set aside on kitchen paper.

Meanwhile, place the pork, Chinese five spice powder and 1 teaspoon salt in a bowl and mix well.

Heat a large non-stick frying pan, add the vegetable oil, then add the pork mixture. As the pork heats up, break it up with a wooden spoon or spatula, until the meat is all loose and cooking nicely. You will find that the meat starts to boil, this is quite normal. Let it boil, stirring all the time. After a few minutes, the water will evaporate and the pork will start to cook in the small amount of oil, plus the fat from the pork.

Once the pork is really brown and crispy, after about 5 minutes, spoon it into a colander over a bowl to catch the fat and oil. Discard the excess fat. Season the pork well.

Next, make the dressing by placing the honey, lemon zest and juice, oil, molasses, tamari, sugar, a little salt and pepper into a bowl and whisk well.

Place the lettuce, mouli, pepperdew peppers and watercress together in a large bowl and spoon over the dressing, mix carefully. Add the warm crispy pork and again mix well, but carefully. Divide between 4 plates and top with the crunchy bacon. Serve straight away.

STUFFED CELERY STICKS WITH PARMA HAM

This snack is a simple throwback to the 70s - simple and really tasty, not everybody's cup of tea, but I love it!

1 tablespoon olive oil

4 slices Parma ham, cut into fine strips

1 head of celery

200g herb garlic cream cheese

1 tablespoon gluten-free pesto

2 tablespoons double cream

10 basil leaves, torn

2 tablespoons snipped fresh chives

2 tablespoons chopped fresh coriander

salt and freshly ground black pepper

cayenne pepper, to garnish

Heat the oil in a frying pan, add the Parma ham and cook until crispy.

Cut the celery sticks, on a slight angle, into 10cm long pieces.

Mix the cheese and pesto with enough cream to soften. Stir in the fresh herbs and season well with salt and pepper.

Pipe or spread the herby cheese into the celery sticks, top with the cooked Parma ham and dust with a little cayenne pepper.

MARINATED SMOKED SALMON WITH PICKLED GINGER

SERVES: 6-8 as a starter
PREPARATION: 25mins plus 1 hour marinating
COOKING: 1 hour

I really like the combination of beetroot and salmon - cooked or raw, they both work really well. Add to that pickled ginger, tamari (Japanese soy sauce) and the sharp flavour of the radish and you have a lovely fresh starter for 6-8 or a main course for 4.

For the salad
2 medium beetroots, thoroughly washed
280g smoked salmon
150g mouli (Japanese white radish)
juice of ½ lemon
freshly ground black pepper

For the dressing
150ml rice vinegar
4 tablespoons tamari or gluten-free soy sauce
1 tablespoon caster sugar
1 tablespoon very finely chopped pickled ginger
pickled ginger and tamari or gluten-free soy sauce, to serve

Preheat the oven to 200°C/400°F/gas mark 6. Wrap the beetroots well in two layers of foil. Place on a baking tray and cook in the oven for 1 hour, or until a knife can pass through easily.

Once cooked, peel the beetroot whilst still warm, then set aside to cool.

Meanwhile, finely slice the salmon and place into a bowl.

Peel the mouli, then slice it very finely into thin shreds and add to the salmon.

Cut the peeled beetroot into thin strips and add to the salmon.

Sprinkle over the lemon juice and add a little pepper, mix well, but carefully, as the cooked beetroot will break up easily.

Mix all the dressing ingredients together, then pour over the salmon. Stir well, then leave for 1 hour at room temperature.

Serve with extra pickled ginger and tamari or soy sauce on the side.

SERVES: 4–6
PREPARATION: 30mins
COOKING: 4–5mins

SPICY FALAFEL WITH YOGURT AND HONEY DIP

I first cooked this recipe right on the shores of the Dead Sea in Israel and since then it has become a bit of a favourite. If you have a small, spring-loaded falafel press to mould them with, then so much the better. However, if not, don't worry – I often use two teaspoons. The important thing is to cook in small batches.

225g chickpeas, soaked overnight
4 garlic cloves, finely chopped
2 teaspoons sesame seeds
1 small onion, finely chopped
1 teaspoon paprika
1 teaspoon cumin
4 tablespoons chopped fresh coriander
4 tablespoons chopped fresh flat-leaf parsley
½ teaspoon salt
1 level teaspoon ground black pepper
2–4 tablespoons gluten-free breadcrumbs

vegetable oil
1 teaspoon bicarbonate of soda

For the yogurt
225g thick natural yogurt
1 teaspoon ground turmeric
1 teaspoon ground cumin
1 teaspoon sesame seeds
2 teaspoons caster sugar
4 tablespoons finely chopped fresh coriander
2–3 tablespoons honey

Rinse the soaked chickpeas under cold running water, then place in a food processor with the garlic, sesame seeds, onion, paprika, cumin and herbs and blitz until you have a slightly rough texture. Add a little water if you need to loosen the mixture a little.

Transfer to a large bowl, season and add enough breadcrumbs so that the falafel mix holds together (don't go mad and add all at once). Cover the bowl and place in the fridge to chill for about 20 minutes or so.

To make the yogurt dip, simply mix all the ingredients together and place in the fridge as I like to serve it chilled.

When you are ready to cook the falafel, heat 3–4cm of oil to 185°C in a large pan and stir the bicarbonate of soda into the falafel mix.

Using a falafel mould or two teaspoons, shape the mixture into small, flattened balls and deep-fry in the pan until golden brown. (I recommend you fry 6–8 at a time.)

When cooked, drain well on kitchen paper and serve immediately (some insist within 90 seconds of cooking!) together with the yogurt dip.

ROAST CHICKEN STOCK WITH FRESH PARSLEY AND LEMON

SERVES: 4
PREPARATION: 15mins
COOKING: 50mins

I think we waste too much these days, so this recipe is for a Sunday night or a Monday evening to use up the carcass from roast chicken.

1 roasted chicken carcass, cut into pieces

1.8 litres cold water

1 x 10g gluten-free chicken stock cube

1 large carrot, finely diced

1 large onion, finely chopped

½ red chilli, finely chopped (optional)

1 large courgette, finely diced

handful of frozen peas

1 fresh or dried bay leaf

stalks from a bunch of fresh parsley

a few black peppercorns

3 garlic cloves, crushed

1 tablespoon cornflour or arrowroot stirred into
a little cold water zest of 1 lemon

1 tablespoon lemon juice

1 small bunch of basil, roughly chopped

salt and freshly ground black pepper

Place the carcass and water in a large saucepan. Sprinkle over the stock cube and bring to the boil. Reduce the heat and simmer nice and slowly for about 35 minutes.

When the stock is cooked strain it through a fine sieve and leave it to stand for about 10 minutes.

Using a ladle or tablespoon, skim off all the visible fat from the stock then transfer the stock to a clean saucepan.

Add the carrot, onion and chilli, if using, and bring back to the boil and simmer for about 10 minutes until the vegetables are tender but not overcooked.

At this point add the courgette, peas, bay leaf, parsley, peppercorns and garlic, then simmer for about 1 minute so the vegetables keep their colour.

Whilst the stock is still boiling add the cornflour paste and stir thoroughly to thicken. The stock should still be quite thin; if it thickens too much add a little boiling water.

Finally, add the lemon zest and juice and basil. Season to taste with salt and pepper and serve in deep bowls.

BASMATI RICE AND PARMESAN SPOON BREAD

I spent a lot of time in the USA in the 90s where I discovered this really tasty bread-come-frittata recipe. Serve it with smoked salmon and cream cheese for breakfast, as a light lunch with some gluten-free baked beans or even with roast chicken breasts or fillet steak. It's delicious – try it!

1 x 250g packet microwaveable plain boiled rice

350ml milk

½ teaspoon salt

½ teaspoon ground black pepper

75g Parmesan cheese, grated

55g unsalted butter, melted

5 medium eggs, separated

20g chives or spring onions, chopped

pinch of cream of tartar

1½ teaspoons xanthan gum

1 teaspoon arrowroot

Preheat the oven to 180°C/350°F/gas mark 4. Lightly oil a 30cm round, 3cm deep pizza tray or baking dish.

Microwave the rice following the packet instructions. Place the rice in a pan, with the milk, 200ml water and the salt and pepper and bring to the boil. Reduce the heat and simmer for 15–20 minutes, or until you can draw a spoon through the mixture and it will stay apart. Spoon into a bowl and cool slightly.

Once cooled, add the cheese, melted butter, egg yolks and chives or spring onions and mix well. Whisk the egg whites and cream of tartar together until the mixture is creamy and thick, do not overwhisk.

Add the xanthan gum and arrowroot to the rice mixture and mix well, then add the egg whites, mix well, then season again if needed.

Pour into the prepared tin and cook for 20–25 minutes, until set and lightly browned. Cool slightly, then carefully turn out onto a wire cooling rack.

The bread can be eaten cut into wedges, at room temperature or well chilled.

JUICY CHICKEN BITES WITH GREEN HORSERADISH MAYO

SERVES: 10
PREPARATION: 45mins plus at least 1 hour marinating
COOKING: 8-10mins

This takes a little time but is well worth the effort. The tasty little chicken bites will fall off the bone and work really well with a tangy mayonnaise flavoured with wasabi (Japanese green horseradish paste). Great snack or canapé food!

32 chicken wings

4 tablespoons gluten-free tomato ketchup

2 tablespoons red wine vinegar

2 tablespoons dark brown sugar

4 teaspoons gluten-free English mustard powder

pinch of chilli powder

dash of gluten-free Worcestershire sauce

4 garlic cloves, crushed

2 tablespoons olive oil

2 tablespoons tamarind paste

1 teaspoon ground cumin

1 teaspoon ground coriander

8 tablespoons mayonnaise (check it is a gluten-free variety)

2 teaspoons wasabi

4 tablespoons chopped fresh parsley

4 tablespoons chopped fresh basil

4 tablespoons chopped fresh coriander

salt

Lay a chicken wing flat on a chopping board and with a sharp knife cut the tip, and the bottom knuckle off the wing, cutting through two bones at either end. Keep the bits and pieces in the freezer for when you make the next soup or stock.

Push the smaller of the bones out from one end and it will slide out easily. You should end up with a clean bone and a nice small piece of chicken at one end. Repeat with the remaining wings.

Make up the marinade by whisking together the ketchup, vinegar, sugar, mustard, chilli, Worcestershire sauce or alternative, garlic, oil, tamarind paste, ground cumin and ground coriander and mix well. Season with a little salt, add the wings and mix well. Leave for 1 hour or best overnight.

Preheat the oven to 220°C/425°F/gas mark 7. Place the chicken in a large roasting tin and roast for about 8-10 minutes until cooked through and golden and sticky.

Make up the mayo by mixing the mayonnaise, wasabi, parsley and basil together. Arrange the cooked chicken on a serving dish and sprinkle over the chopped coriander. Serve the mayo separately. Perfect finger food!

SERVES: 4
PREPARATION: 30mins
COOKING: 20mins

POPCORN CHICKEN WITH SPICY DIPPING SAUCE

This is a really good way of eating white meats such as chicken, turkey and even guinea fowl. The secret is to use condensed milk in the coating – it really adds to the flavour and richness of the meat, trust me! I had a fried chicken dish in Tennessee many years ago and when I enquired why the chicken was so succulent, the chef told me that he marinated the meat in condensed milk. I laughed, but I tried it and it made all the difference; give it a go and you'll see what I mean!

For the sauce

350ml mayonnaise (check it is a gluten-free variety)

2 teaspoons roughly chopped fresh chilli

3 teaspoons gluten-free Dijon mustard

juice and zest of 1 large lime

2 large spring onions, roughly chopped

4 teaspoons chopped gherkins

3 tablespoons chopped fresh tarragon

100g finely chopped roasted red peppers from a jar

4 tablespoons roughly chopped fresh parsley

4 teaspoons sugar

salt and freshly ground black pepper

For the chicken

2 medium chicken or pheasant breasts, skinned

3 tablespoons condensed milk

2 medium eggs, lightly beaten

pinch dried chilli powder

½ teaspoon ground cumin

2 tablespoons cornflour

6–8 tablespoons fine cornmeal or polenta

rapeseed oil, for deep frying

Mix all the ingredients for the dipping sauce in a bowl and set aside.

Cut the chicken or pheasant into 2cm cubes, removing any sinew from the fillet and inner breast.

In a shallow dish, mix the condensed milk with the eggs and 2 tablespoons water. Season with the chilli powder, cumin and plenty of black pepper. Place the cornflour on a plate and the cornmeal or polenta on a separate plate.

First coat the chicken pieces in the cornflour. Next place them in the egg mixture and coat well. Finally drop the small nuggets into the cornmeal and coat thoroughly.

Fill a deep frying pan with 2cm of rapeseed oil, then heat to 170°C/325°F or until a cube of bread browns in 15 seconds. Fry the chicken in small batches until golden brown, place the cooked chicken on a warm plate, covered in foil, to keep hot. Drain well, then sprinkle with a little salt. Serve the hot popcorn chicken with the sauce on the side .

QUICK TOFU MISO SOUP

SERVES: 4
PREPARATION: 5mins
COOKING: none

I really like miso soup; I always feel like it's doing me some good and it's a lovely way to start a meal – full of flavour and texture. The secret is to serve it straight away so the vegetables are nice and crisp. An extra dash or two of tamari always goes down well.

4 x 10g sachets gluten-free instant miso

900ml boiling water

100g smoked tofu, cubed

4 tablespoons tamari

50g shiitake mushrooms, finely sliced

50g closed button mushrooms, finely sliced

1 tablespoon fresh ginger, peeled and finely chopped

10g nori (dried seaweed), very finely shredded

3 spring onions, finely sliced on the diagonal

Make up the instant miso sachets with boiling water, following the pack instructions.

Mix all the rest of the ingredients together in a bowl. Then divide equally between 4 bowls or cups.

Carefully ladle over the hot miso, then serve.

BORLOTTI BEAN, CHILLI AND PINE NUT BAKE

This recipe works well with gluten-free pasta, which is available from most supermarkets. The secret is to lightly cook the pasta, then finish cooking it in the oven. You can cover it with mozzarella or Parmesan for a cheesy topping. Or just pop it in the oven without any cheese for a crunchy topping.

200g gluten-free pasta shapes

2 tablespoons olive oil

1 x 425g can borlotti beans, well drained

finely grated zest of 1 large lemon

40g pine nuts

4 tablespoons roughly chopped fresh parsley

pinch or two of dried chilli flakes

350ml double cream

½ x 10g gluten-free vegetable stock cube

200g mozzarella cheese, sliced or 50g Parmesan cheese, grated (optional)

salt and freshly ground black pepper

green salad with rocket and onion, to serve

Preheat the oven to 220ºC/425ºF/gas mark 7.

Cook the pasta for half the time stated on the pack. Drain well. Toss in the olive oil to stop the pasta sticking together.

Meanwhile, place the beans, lemon zest, pine nuts, parsley and chilli in a bowl and mix well. Add the pasta to the bean mixture.

Place the cream and stock cube in a small pan, bring to the boil, whisk well to dissolve the cube, then pour over the bean mixture and stir well. Taste, then season if needed.

Spoon the mixture into a 28 x 28 x 4cm baking dish. Top with the sliced mozzarella or grated Parmesan, if using, and cook for 20-25 minutes or until well browned.

Once cooked, remove from the oven and cool for 5 minutes before eating, or it will be too hot! Serve with a green salad with plenty of onion and rocket.

SERVES: 4
PREPARATION: 20mins
COOKING: 15-20mins

PASTA GRATIN WITH PEPPERS AND SMOKED GARLIC

The general rule of thumb is raw pasta will yield roughly 1½ times the weight when cooked. So in this recipe, 500g will give you roughly 800g, give or take a little, depending on the absorption rate of different makes of dried pasta. In this recipe you should end up with a fairly moist end result with a slightly crunchy top where the pasta pokes through the sauce and cheese. My kids love pasta bakes.

40ml olive oil

2 medium onions, finely chopped

4 cloves smoked garlic, chopped

500g rice and corn pasta

2 large yellow peppers, chopped into 2cm dice

1 x 10g gluten-free vegetable stock cube

450ml whipping cream

40g fresh basil, chopped

50g Parmesan cheese, grated

50g gluten-free breadcrumbs or crushed rice crackers

salt and freshly ground black pepper

green salad, to serve

Preheat the oven to 200°C/400°F/gas mark 6.

Heat the oil in a frying pan, then add the onions and garlic and cook for 10 minutes until softened.

Cook the pasta according to the packet instructions. Once cooked, drain and spoon into a baking dish, approximately 22 x 30 x 7cm.

Add the peppers and the crumbled stock cube to the onions and garlic, stir in the cream and then cook for 15–20 minutes over a gentle heat until you have about 900g of sauce. The peppers should be very soft at this point. Season to taste.

Stir the basil into the sauce and then pour it over the cooked pasta. Stir well and top with the Parmesan cheese.

Sprinkle with the gluten-free breadcrumbs or crushed rice cakes and bake for 15–20 minutes until browned. Serve with a green salad.

FERN'S HONEYED BAKED BEANS ON MUSTARD DROP SCONES

SERVES: 4
PREPARATION: 15mins
COOKING: 10mins

This is Fern's recipe and it's really delicious! I get a real kick out of cooking simple shop-bought ingredients with a twist but have had to 'perfect' her idea a little! Well, I am a chef after all!

For the scones

40g cornflour

100g chestnut or chickpea (gram) flour

2 pinches of cream of tartar

2 pinches of bicarbonate of soda

1 medium egg, lightly beaten

2 tablespoons gluten-free wholegrain mustard

6 tablespoons milk (approximately)

2 tablespoons chopped fresh coriander

2 tablespoons vegetable oil, for shallow frying

salt and freshly ground black pepper

For the beans

1 x 410g can gluten-free baked beans

15g unsalted butter

½ teaspoon dried red chilli flakes

1 tablespoon clear honey

4 tablespoons chopped fresh coriander

clear honey and fresh coriander, to serve (optional)

Place the cornflour, chestnut or chickpea flour, cream of tartar and bicarbonate of soda in a bowl and mix well. Add a pinch or two of salt and a little pepper.

Add the egg and mustard and mix well, and then add enough milk to form a thickish batter – about the consistency of thick double cream. Finally, add the chopped coriander.

Heat the vegetable oil in a non-stick frying pan. Place 2–3 tablespoons of batter in the hot pan. Cook the scones for 2–3 minutes until the sides and top are just set, then flip over and cook for a further 1–2 minutes to set. Once cooked, place on a warm plate and cover with foil to keep hot. Repeat until all the batter is used up – you should have 8–10 scones.

Warm the beans in a small pan and add the butter, chilli and honey. Once the beans are hot and the butter has melted, stir in the fresh coriander until it wilts.

Serve the warm drop scones topped with a good spoonful of beans and a little extra honey and coriander if you want.

STIR-FRIED RICE WITH AVOCADO AND HORSERADISH

Fried rice with a difference - quick, easy and filling. This was really my wife's idea so I can't take the credit!

2 x 115g packs microwaveable basmati rice

2 large tomatoes, chopped

1 ripe avocado, cubed

4 tablespoons chopped fresh coriander

2 spring onions, sliced diagonally

1-2 tablespoons vegetable oil

2 large eggs, beaten

1 tablespoon creamed horseradish

salt and freshly ground black pepper

Cook the rice in the microwave for 2 minutes.

Place the tomatoes, avocado, coriander and spring onions in a serving dish and mix well.

Heat the oil in a wok, add the warmed rice and stir well.

Add the beaten eggs and mix well until the eggs are cooked. Season well with salt and pepper.

Tip the rice onto the tomato mixture, season well and stir in the creamed horseradish. Serve straight away, whilst hot.

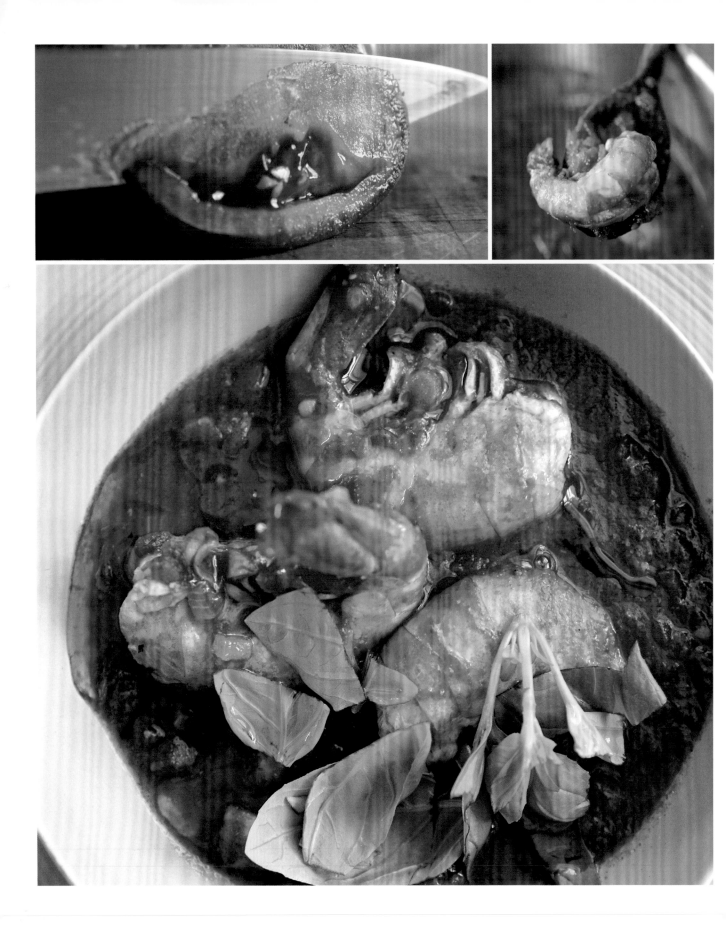

SIMPLE TOMATO, PRAWN AND OUZO STEW

SERVES: 4
PREPARATION: 10mins
COOKING: 25mins

I went to Greece years ago and had a delicious dish of butter beans stewed with freshwater prawns, fresh tomatoes and ouzo – a Pernod-like Greek spirit – and it was delicious. I brought a bottle back, and like most people chucked it in the cupboard and forgot all about it. Then I dusted it off one day thinking, I'll use that at some point. That point came when I decided to put this recipe in the book.

Pernod is a perfectably acceptable alternative to ouzo, but take care – a little is all you need. I should also mention here that I cook with ordinary olive or rapeseed oil, then finish with extra virgin oil, keeping the best for flavouring.

2 tablespoons olive or rapeseed oil

1 large onion, finely chopped

1 small glass ouzo or Pernod

2 x 410g cans chopped tomatoes

2 large fresh tomatoes, chopped

1 x 10g gluten-free fish stock cube

2 teaspoons sugar

4 tablespoons chopped fresh basil

300g frozen prawns

2 tablespoons extra virgin olive oil

salt and freshly ground black pepper

steamed rice, to serve

Heat the olive or rapeseed oil in a large pan, then add the onion and cook for 5 minutes.

Add the ouzo or Pernod, bring to the boil and simmer for 2 minutes.

Add the canned tomatoes, fresh tomatoes, stock cube, sugar and seasoning to the pan.

Stir well and cook for 15 minutes, or until you have a nice, thick stew.

Add the basil, prawns and extra virgin olive oil to the pan, and heat through until piping hot. Be careful not to overcook the prawns.

Serve with a glass of dry white wine and a little steamed rice.

SERVES: 8
PREPARATION: 20mins
COOKING: 25mins

SAUTÉED CHICKEN LIVERS WITH TARRAGON MUFFINS

Baking without gluten makes it extremely difficult to get structure into breads, cakes and muffins. Here the combination of baking powder and the paper cases to hold up the muffins gives a pretty good finished result. The texture will be open and crumbly, but that's fine as we have a lovely, creamy sauce to soak into the muffin.

For the muffins

150g fine cornmeal or polenta

2 teaspoons gluten-free baking powder

75g chestnut flour

4 tablespoons olive oil

1 medium egg

275ml milk

100g tinned or frozen sweetcorn (defrosted)

4 tablespoons roughly chopped fresh tarragon

salt and freshly ground black pepper

For the liver

300g whole chicken livers, fresh or defrosted

50g unsalted butter

100ml Madeira

150ml double cream

Preheat the oven to 200°C/400°F/gas mark 6. Place 8 paper muffin cases in a muffin tray. Place the cornmeal or polenta, baking powder, chestnut flour, salt and pepper in a large mixing bowl and stir well together.

Place the oil, egg and milk in a jug and whisk well. Pour the oil mixture into the dry ingredients and stir well; then add the sweetcorn and tarragon. The mixture should be soft but not too runny, or too thick. Spoon the mixture into the muffin cases in the muffin tray, then cook for 20–25 minutes, or until well risen and golden.

Meanwhile, pick over the livers, and remove any green stained marks, or membranes. Cut each lobe (that's the cheffy name for two halves of the liver) into two.

Melt the unsalted butter in a non-stick frying pan, until slightly golden and bubbling. Add the livers and gently sauté on one side for 2–3 minutes, then flip over, add the Madeira and bring to the boil, cook for 2 minutes, then add the cream. Swirl around, and add a little salt and pepper to taste.

Do not overcook the livers; they should be rose pink when cut open. Once the muffins are cooked, remove from the cases and split in half. Arrange cut-side up on 8 plates and top with the creamy livers.

SIMPLE SPICED FRIED CHICKEN

SERVES: 4
PREPARATION: 10mins
COOKING: 10mins

This is another simple recipe that will give you great results. Make sure the meat is coated well not only in the spice, garlic and tamari but also in the egg white and flour in order to ensure it all cooks evenly. Also, fry in small batches so the oil remains nice and hot.

For the chicken

8 chicken thighs, deboned and skin discarded
2 teaspoons Chinese five-spice powder
2 garlic cloves, crushed, then really finely pasted
2 tablespoons tamari
1 medium egg white, lightly beaten
salt and freshly ground black pepper
250g tapioca or cornflour (approx)
700ml vegetable oil
1 teaspoon Chinese five-spice powder
finely grated zest and juice of 1 lime

For the salad

4 tablespoons chopped fresh mint
4 large plum tomatoes, chopped
2 small Little Gem lettuces, roughly chopped
1 large pomegranate, seeded
4 tablespoons chopped fresh Thai basil
salt and freshly ground black pepper

First make the salad. Place all the ingredients in a large bowl and toss together.

Using a sharp knife, cut the chicken into 2cm slices, then place in a bowl with the five-spice powder and toss to coat.

Add the garlic, tamari and egg white and mix well, then season with salt and pepper. Shake off any excess coating and lightly toss in the tapioca or cornflour.

Heat the oil in a wok or deep saucepan (so it is about 4-6cm deep) to 190°C (or when the oil starts to bubble around an inserted wooden spoon). Transfer the chicken straight into the hot oil and cook until crispy and golden brown.

Drain the fried chicken on kitchen paper and season with a little salt and pepper, more five-spice powder and a squeeze of lime. Serve immediately with the salad.

OUTDOORS

SERVES: 4
PREPARATION: 30mins
plus marinating time
COOKING: 15mins

JAPANESE SALMON WITH FRESH MINT CHUTNEY

The flavours here are really intense - the salmon is sweet and succulent, whilst the chutney is minty and powerful and together they are very well matched. If you can leave the salmon to marinate overnight, all the better. I cook down the rest of the marinade that is left over to use as a dipping sauce.

4 x 175g salmon fillets, skinned

Steamed Pak Choi, to serve (see below)

For the mint chutney

60g fresh mint leaves, washed well

2 large, ripe tomatoes, chopped

2 heaped teaspoons chopped green chilli

5 garlic cloves, finely chopped

2 tablespoons olive oil

juice of ½ lime

salt and freshly ground black pepper

For the marinade

200ml mirin (sweet fermented Japanese rice liqueur)

150ml tamari (Japanese soy sauce) or gluten-free soy sauce

1 tablespoon toasted sesame oil

2 tablespoons caster sugar

2 tablespoons sherry vinegar

Place the mint, tomatoes, chilli, garlic and olive oil in a liquidiser or food processor. Blitz until you have a nice purée, not too chunky, or too smooth. Spoon into a bowl, then add the lime juice and seasoning to taste.

Place the mirin, tamari, sesame oil, sugar and vinegar in a small saucepan, mix well, then bring to the boil. Turn down the heat and simmer the sauce until it has reduced by about half. Remove from the heat and set aside to cool. Once cooled, pour the marinade over the salmon and leave to marinate for at least 1 hour in the fridge.

To cook the salmon, preheat the grill to its hottest setting. Lift out the salmon, leaving a little sauce on the fish, then place on a grill tray or heatproof dish. Cook for 8–10 minutes, depending on the temperature of the grill, or until the salmon is just cooked - it should feel firm to the touch.

Meanwhile, boil the rest of the marinade that is left, and serve with the salmon as a dipping sauce. Serve the salmon with the sauce and the chutney and Steamed Pak Choi.

Steamed Pak Choi: place 4 well-washed pak choi on a large plate. Season well with salt and pepper. Cover with clingfilm, make a few incisions, and microwave on High for 6 minutes. Once cooked, remove, uncover, drain off the water and serve with the salmon.

SWEET PICKLED MACKEREL WITH HERBS

SERVES: 4
PREPARATION: 15mins plus 24 hours chilling time
COOKING: 25mins

This is a perfect, tasty, colourful spring or summer dish. Having said that, it also works well in the winter months. The secret is to remove the fish from the fridge 20 minutes before eating – the flavours will develop remarkably in that time.

4 tablespoons olive oil

1 small onion, finely sliced

2 garlic cloves, crushed

1 large carrot, finely sliced

1 glass white wine vinegar

1 glass dry white wine

1 glass water

2 fresh bay leaves

1 teaspoon sea salt

2 teaspoons caster sugar

pinch red chilli flakes

pinch ground white pepper

2 tablespoons lemon juice

1 teaspoon chopped fresh marjoram

1 tablespoon chopped flat leaf parsley

4 large mackerel fillets, boned

rocket leaves and sliced gluten-free sourdough bread, to serve

Heat the oil and fry the onion, garlic and carrot until softened.

Add the rest of the ingredients, except the mackerel, taste and then simmer for about 20 minutes; do not overcook.

Carefully remove the outer skin of the mackerel, using your fingers.

Place the fillets in a steel, glass or earthenware dish, then pour over the hot pickling liquid. Cool and chill in the fridge for 24 hours.

Serve with a little rocket and a couple of slices of sourdough bread. Drizzle over a little more oil if needed.

SERVES: 6
PREPARATION: 20mins
COOKING: 45-50mins

QUICK PORK CHOPS WITH BUTTERNUT RELISH

This recipe is amazing for bringing out the flavour of the pork. Marinating in a simple brine for a few minutes can make all the difference to the succulence of pork, chicken and turkey. Serve with a few new potatoes and green beans.

For the pork

6 x 140g pork chops, rind scored in 1cm slices

oil, for brushing

For the brine

30g caster sugar

15g salt

For the butternut relish

4 tablespoons olive oil

1 teaspoon caraway seeds

1 teaspoon whole cloves

1 small red onion, finely chopped

2 garlic cloves, crushed

1 tablespoon finely chopped fresh root ginger

450g butternut squash, peeled, deseeded and
  roughly cubed

125ml red wine vinegar

2 tablespoons balsamic vinegar

1 tablespoon gluten-free Worcestershire sauce

175g light brown muscovado sugar

salt and freshly ground black pepper

For the glaze

3 tablespoons maple syrup

1½ tablespoons olive oil

new potatoes and green beans, to serve

First, prepare the relish. Heat the olive oil in a large pan. Add the caraway seeds, cloves, onions, garlic and ginger and cook for about 6-8 minutes.

Add the squash, vinegars, Worcestershire sauce and sugar, stir and season well. Cover and cook slowly, until the squash is tender, this should take about 10 minutes. Then remove the lid and cook until pulpy and thick, about 10 minutes.

To make the brine, place the sugar, salt and 300ml cold water in a small pan and heat until the sugar and salt have dissolved. Pour into a measuring jug and top up to 350ml with cold water. Place the chops in a single layer in a non-metallic dish and pour the brine over. Leave to marinate for 10-15 minutes.

Preheat the grill to medium, and brush the chops with a little oil on both sides. Combine the maple syrup and olive oil to make the glaze. Grill the chops for 5-6 minutes on each side then, when just cooked, finally brush with the maple syrup and olive oil mixture. Return to the grill for 1-2 minutes, taking care as they will catch very easily. Serve with the relish.

GRILLED CHICKEN CHOPS WITH RED PEPPER MAYO

This is a bit different - yes a chicken chop! It's easy to prepare and 4 large thighs will feed 4 adults easily. Served simply with a blob of roast pepper mayo, watercress and fresh ripe mango it makes a flavour-packed main course.

For the chicken

4 large skinless, bone-in chicken thighs

2 tablespoons olive oil

juice of ½ lime

salt and freshly ground black pepper

For the mayo

350ml mayonnaise (check it is a gluten-free variety)

2 teaspoons roughly chopped fresh chilli

3 teaspoons gluten-free Dijon mustard

juice of 1 large lime

2 large spring onions, roughly chopped

4 teaspoons chopped gherkins

3 tablespoons chopped fresh tarragon

3 teaspoons Cajun spice mix (check it is a gluten-free variety)

4 teaspoons sugar

6 tablespoons roughly chopped fresh coriander

200g roasted red peppers (from a jar), finely chopped

1 large, ripe mango, peeled and thinly sliced, 1 large bunch watercress and lime wedges, to serve

Preheat the barbecue or grill to medium. To prepare each chop, lay the thigh flat on a chopping board. Carefully, cut down each side of the bone, leaving a little meat attached.

Next, run the knife around the bone, gently freeing it from the flesh, taking care to not cut through the bottom 1cm. Unfold the meat and lay it out flat, leaving the bone attached, so it looks like a chop. Pat flat with a large knife.

Mix the mayo, chilli, mustard, lime juice and spring onions together. Next, add the gherkins, tarragon, spice mix and sugar, then taste and adjust the seasoning if needed. Finally, add the coriander and roasted peppers to the mayo, mix, then chill until ready.

Rub the chicken chops with the olive oil and lime juice and seasoning. Lightly cook the chops on the barbecue or under the grill for 6-8 minutes on each side, turning once. The chops are cooked if the juices run clear when the thickest part of the chicken is pierced with a knife. Once cooked, remove from the barbecue or grill, and keep warm.

Divide the mango between 4 plates, then top with a little watercress. Add a chicken chop and a nice blob of red pepper mayo. Serve with the lime wedges.

NAKED BEEF BURGERS

SERVES: 6
PREPARATION: 10mins
COOKING: 8-12mins

Naked, purely because they have no salt and pepper! But you can add as much or as little as you want, if preferred. My friend Polly from The Fine Beef Company sells naked burgers, and they not only out-sell all the other flavours, but sell all year round.

500g minced beef (15-20 per cent fat content)
3 tablespoons gluten-free breadcrumbs
vegetable oil, for cooking
salt and freshly ground black pepper (optional)
burger buns, to serve (optional)

The secrets of a good burger are to:
1) use minced, or ground as the Americans call it, chuck steak - 8mm mincing-plate size is perfect
2) use meat that has between 15-20 per cent fat
3) and mince the meat twice, then mix together well, the meat will bind easier and the burger will hold its fat and moisture better.

Just mix the beef and breadcrumbs well together, and add salt and pepper if you want to.

Roll into 6 equal-sized balls, and then flatten. Preheat the barbecue or grill to medium.

Very lightly oil the burgers on both sides; also lightly oil the barbecue rack using kitchen paper.

Grill the burgers for 2-3 minutes, then turn them through 90° (this will give them an attractive criss-cross effect) and continue to cook for a further couple of minutes. Flip over and cook for the same amount of time on the second side.

Serve the burgers on their own or in a bun.

SERVES: 6
PREPARATION: 20mins
plus chilling time
COOKING: 10–12mins

JUICY TURKEY BASIL AND CORN BURGERS

I think leg or brown meat on turkey makes better burgers, purely because the meat is juicier. Breast meat is fine also, and is extremely good for you, but needs a little more attention when preparing and cooking. Skinned turkey breast can be less than 2 per cent fat, so when it cooks, it can cook slightly drier, leaving you with a crumbly texture. But I have discovered a great trick - if you add just a little mayonnaise, it really helps to keep the burger beautifully juicy and tasty.

500g minced turkey (preferably leg meat)

2 tablespoons mayonnaise (check it is a gluten-free variety)

2 tablespoons chopped fresh basil

2 tablespoons gluten-free Worcestershire sauce

½ medium egg white, lightly beaten

2 heaped tablespoons tinned sweetcorn, well drained

2-3 tablespoons brown rice flour or polenta

olive oil, for frying

salt and ground white pepper

iceberg lettuce, sliced ripe tomato and Mango Mint Dressing (see opposite), to serve

Place the turkey, mayo, basil, Worcestershire sauce and egg white in a bowl. Stir really well, then add the sweetcorn and brown rice flour or polenta, season and mix well again.

Leave to chill for 30 minutes.

Mould the mixture into 6 balls, flatten slightly into small patties, then re-chill for 5–10 minutes. Preheat the barbecue or grill to medium.

To cook, lightly spray the patties with a little olive oil (I use a plant mister filled with oil) then spray the barbecue rack quickly before you cook the burgers; this will stop them from sticking.

Cook the burgers for 3-4 minutes, then turn through 90° – this will give an attractive criss-cross effect. Cook for a further 3-4 minutes. Turn the burgers over and cook for a further 3-4 minutes.

Serve with a little chopped iceberg lettuce, sliced ripe tomato and a spoonful or two of Mango Mint Dressing (see recipe opposite).

MANGO MINT DRESSING

SERVES: 6
PREPARATION: 10mins
COOKING: none

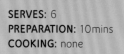

Canned mango is a great store cupboard back-up; it tastes delicious and makes a great sauce. I picked this idea up from my friend who has an Indian takeaway! It works really well with the turkey burgers.

1 x 400g tin mango, drained (reserve the syrup)
200g thick Greek yogurt
2-3 tablespoons mango syrup from the can
1 tablespoon roughly chopped fresh mint
2 tablespoons white wine vinegar
salt and freshly ground black pepper

Place all the ingredients in a liquidiser, season and blitz until smooth. Add a little more syrup if needed, but the dressing should have a thickish consistency.

STICKY CHICKEN WITH TWICE COOKED BAKED POTATOES

SERVES: 4
PREPARATION: 20mins
COOKING: 30mins

This sticky lime sauce is so tasty and it really lifts the flavour of the chicken. It's simple to make, and you get two uses - a sticky marinade and a dipping sauce. I make no apologies for using ready-prepared garlic and ginger - they're great, especially if you're in a hurry.

4 skinned chicken breasts

For the sauce
2 tablespoons ready-prepared ginger purée
1 tablespoon ready-prepared garlic purée
4 tablespoons vegetable oil
1 teaspoon Chinese five-spice powder (check it is a gluten-free variety)
½ teaspoon ground cinnamon
½ teaspoon paprika

100ml white wine vinegar
100g muscovado sugar
2 tablespoons clear honey
juice of 6 large limes
1 tablespoon cornflour
salt and freshly ground black pepper

For the potatoes
4 large baked potatoes, cooked and cold
4 sprigs fresh rosemary
4 tablespoons olive oil

Place the ginger purée, garlic purée, vegetable oil, Chinese five-spice powder, cinnamon, paprika, white wine vinegar, sugar, honey, lime juice and seasoning in a large saucepan.

Bring to the boil, then reduce the heat and simmer until thick; this will take about 15-20 minutes. Preheat the oven to 220°C/425°F/gas mark 7.

Cut the cooked baked potatoes in half and score well with a knife. Place some of the fresh rosemary in the score marks, then drizzle over the olive oil and leave to soak in. Season well with salt and pepper.

Fry the potatoes cut-side down in a non-stick frying pan for 5-10 minutes. Then pop them into the oven for 15-20 minutes to crisp up nicely.

Stir the cornflour with a little bit of water in a cup to make a smooth paste. Once the sauce is cooked, stir in the paste to thicken it. Allow the sauce to cool. Place the chicken in an ovenproof dish and spoon half of the sauce over. Reserve the remaining sauce to use as a dip.

Cook the chicken in the oven for 20 minutes, or until glazed, sticky and well coloured. Serve with the twice cooked potatoes and dipping sauce separately.

SERVES: 6–8 as a starter, 4 as a main course
PREPARATION: 15mins
COOKING: none

EASY THAI-STYLE SPICY CRAB PAK CHOI SALAD

I love this salad; it's crisp, tasty and really filling and the powerful flavour of the dressing is fabulous. Serve as a great starter or as a main course. I think the salad also works well with roasted corn-fed chicken breast instead of crab, the sharpness of the dressing cutting the richness of the chicken.

For the salad

8 paper-thin slices of lemon, quartered
100g fine green beans, cut into 2cm pieces
10 cherry plum tomatoes, halved
2 medium carrots, peeled
4 heads pak choi
2 x 240g tins crabmeat, well drained

For the dressing

juice of 3 large limes
3 tablespoons tamarind paste
3 tablespoons Thai fish sauce
2 garlic cloves, finely chopped
2 heaped teaspoons finely chopped red chilli
3 tablespoons tamari
1 tablespoon heaped caster sugar
50ml vegetable oil
salt and ground black pepper (optional)

Place the lemon, beans and tomatoes in a large bowl.

Finely slice the carrots or slice them in a machine or food processor. Add to the bowl and mix well.

Cut the pak choi into 6-8 pieces each, then add to the bowl along with the crabmeat, do not overmix.

Place all the dressing ingredients, apart from the oil, in a small, deep bowl and mix well. Gradually add the oil in a thin stream, whisking all the time.

Pour the dressing over the salad and mix well, taste and season if necessary. I generally find that there is enough seasoning with the tamari and chilli pepper.

Leave for 20 minutes at room temperature then re-mix and serve.

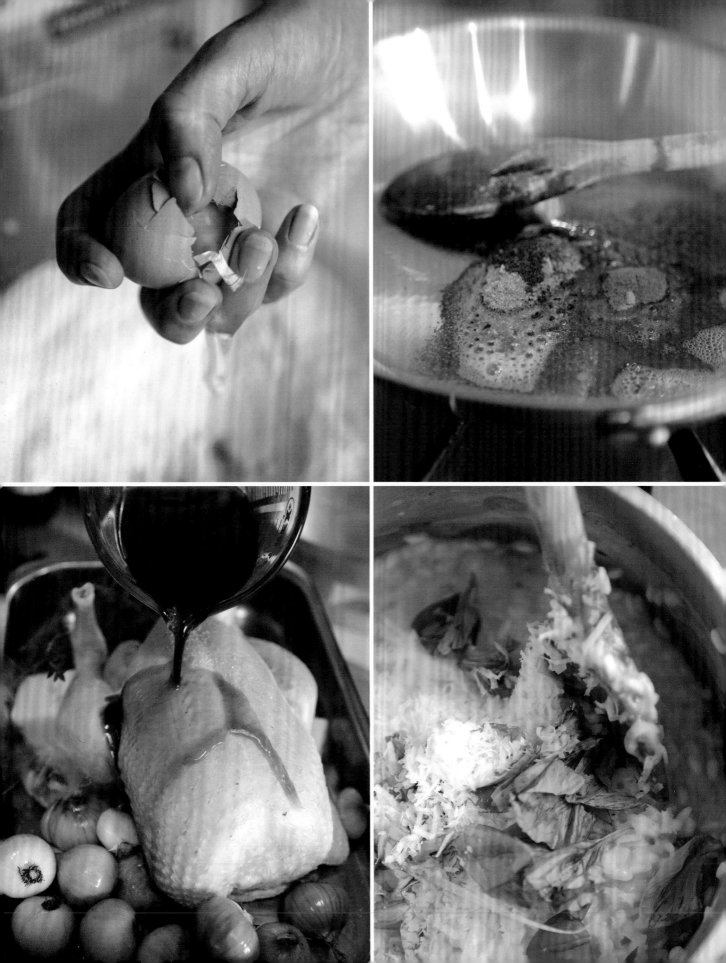

COMFORT

CHESTNUT AND ROASTED ONION BREAD

I could write a whole book on gluten-free bread as it's such a huge subject and very difficult to get the structure just right. However, this chestnut bread is easy and simple to prepare. The sweet roasted onions really help to bring out the nuttiness in the loaf and so this is absolutely the place to start before you build up your breadmaking repertoire.

5 tablespoons olive oil

2 medium onions, finely chopped

3 teaspoons sugar

1 x 7g sachet dried yeast

1 teaspoon xanthan gum

400ml warm water

300g chestnut flour

100g potato flour

½ teaspoon gluten-free baking powder

1 medium egg, lightly beaten

salt and freshly ground black pepper

oil, for greasing

Preheat the oven to 180°C/375°F/gas mark 4. Oil a 900g loaf tin.

Heat 2 tablespoons of the olive oil in a frying pan, then add the onions and 2 teaspoons of sugar. Cook down, stirring occasionally until lightly golden. This will take a few minutes. Once cooked, set aside to cool.

Add the yeast, xanthan gum and the remaining olive oil to the warm water and stir until dissolved.

Combine the flours, onions, remaining sugar, baking powder, 1 teaspoon salt and black pepper in a large bowl and mix well. Add the egg and stir. Next, add the liquid yeast mixture to the bowl and mix well.

Pour into the prepared tin and cook for 30 minutes, or until well risen and lightly browned. Remove and cool slightly, turn out and slice when ready.

CHICKPEA, CHERRY TOMATO AND RICE NOODLE SOUP

I like this soup because it's so easy, no sautéing first – just throw it all in and away you go!

2 garlic cloves, finely chopped

1 teaspoon finely chopped red chilli

1 tablespoon finely chopped ginger

1 small red pepper, finely chopped

½ small leek, finely chopped

100g button mushrooms, very finely sliced

juice of 2 large limes

750ml boiling water

1 x 10g gluten-free vegetable stock cube

50g rice noodles

100ml coconut milk

150g canned chickpeas, well rinsed

12 cherry tomatoes, quartered

4 tablespoons chopped fresh coriander

50g iceberg lettuce, finely shredded

salt and freshly ground black pepper

Place the garlic, chilli, ginger, pepper, leek, mushrooms, lime juice, water and crumbled stock cube in a large saucepan and bring to the boil. Turn down the heat, and simmer for 10 minutes.

Meanwhile, place the rice noodles in a large bowl and cover with boiling water. Leave for 10 minutes to soften, then drain well.

Add the coconut milk to the mushroom stock, bring back to the boil and season to taste.

Add the chickpeas and warm through.

Evenly divide the cooked noodles, cherry tomatoes, coriander and lettuce between 4 bowls. Then ladle in the hot soup and serve.

SOBA NOODLES WITH LIME, COURGETTES AND TURKEY

SERVES: 4
PREPARATION: 10mins
COOKING: 15mins

I love the texture and flavour of Japanese soba noodles, especially when cooked in broths and soups, as they prove how simple cooking can often produce the best results. However, do check they were made in a gluten-free factory as some may otherwise contain traces of gluten.

salt and freshly ground black pepper

200g dried buckwheat soba noodles (I find 50g raw noodles per person is about right, plus check they are a gluten-free variety)

6 tablespoons vegetable oil

350g turkey breast, sliced into 1cm strips

1 large courgette, very finely sliced or julienned

juice of 1 large lime

2 ripe tomatoes, chopped

2 tablespoons chopped fresh basil

a drizzle of extra virgin olive oil (optional)

Bring a medium-sized pan of water to a rolling boil, add a little salt and then plunge in the noodles. Simmer for about 5-6 minutes or until they are soft but not falling apart. Drain well and keep warm.

Meanwhile, heat 3 tablespoons of oil in a non-stick frying pan or wok. Add the turkey strips and gently stir-fry, making sure not to overcook. Transfer to a bowl and set aside.

Place the remaining oil in the pan or wok, add the courgette strips and quickly sauté over a high heat for a minute or so until they wilt. Add the lime juice, turkey and warm noodles and stir to mix well.

Take the pan off the heat, season well with salt and pepper and add the tomatoes and basil. Stir again and add a little extra virgin oil if you like. Serve immediately.

GREEN LENTIL, LIME AND CORIANDER SOUP

The great flavours here make this a really tasty soup. It's nice and easy and is perfect for eating whilst watching your favourite TV programme.

4 tablespoons olive oil

1 medium carrot, finely chopped

2 celery sticks, finely chopped

1 large onion, finely chopped

2 garlic cloves, finely chopped

50g red lentils

2 tablespoons tomato purée

700ml boiling water

1 x 10g gluten-free chicken or vegetable stock cube

100g green lentils

salt and freshly ground black pepper

juice of 2 large limes

3 tablespoons chopped fresh coriander and 100g thick Greek yogurt, to serve

olive oil, to drizzle

Heat the oil in a large pan, then add the carrot, celery, onion and garlic and cook for 5 minutes.

Next, add the red lentils, tomato purée, boiling water and crumbled stock cube and bring to the boil. Turn down the heat and simmer gently until all the vegetables and red lentils are well cooked - about 30 minutes.

Meanwhile, place the green lentils in a saucepan and cover with cold water, bring to the boil and simmer until just cooked, but not falling to pieces. Once cooked, refresh the lentils under cold water.

When the soup is cooked, transfer it in batches to a food processor or liquidiser and process until you have a nice smooth purée. Return the soup to a clean pan. You may need to add a little boiling water if it is too thick. Check the seasoning, then add the lime juice and stir well.

To serve, place the cooked green lentils in 4 bowls. Top with the hot soup, a little fresh coriander and a blob of yogurt swirled in at the last moment. A little olive oil drizzled over is also a nice touch.

LAMB, RED LENTIL AND SWEET POTATO PIE

I'm a big fan of sweet potatoes as they work equally well on their own or with other vegetables. Lentils also add a nice bit of texture to the whole dish and help make the mince go a little further.

500g minced lamb

2 small onions, finely chopped

1 large carrot, roughly chopped

2 teaspoons dried thyme

100g red lentils

600ml water

2 x 10g gluten-free lamb or beef stock cubes

300g potatoes, peeled and chopped

400g sweet potatoes, peeled and chopped

50-75g butter (it's up to you!)

salt and freshly ground black pepper

2 heaped tablespoons soft butter

4 tablespoons gluten-free flour mix (see recipe on page 152)

Place the lamb, onion, carrot, thyme and lentils in a large saucepan, pour in the water, add the crumbled stock cubes, stir to combine and bring to the boil. Simmer for 35-40 minutes or until the lentils and carrots are cooked.

Meanwhile, bring a pan of water to the boil and cook the two potatoes until very soft, then add the butter, salt and pepper and mash together until nice and smooth.

In a small bowl, mix together the butter and flour and then, a little at a time, stir the paste into the simmering mince until it thickens (the mix needs to be fairly thick).

Spoon the mince into a casserole dish and set aside to cool. Once cool, pile on the mash and spread evenly over the surface.

When ready to eat, preheat the oven to 200°C/400°F/gas mark 6 and bake the pie for 25 minutes until golden brown on top and serve with greens of your choice.

SLOW-COOKED INDIAN LAMB KORMA

SERVES: 4-6
PREPARATION: 30mins
COOKING: 4-6 hours in a slow cooker, 4 hours in the oven

This is a great dish to prepare in the slow cooker – just pop it in and it cooks on its own; good food can't get much simpler than that! If you don't own a slow cooker, then follow the same method, but use a deep flameproof casserole dish with a tight-fitting lid and cook at 180°C/350°F/gas mark 4 for 4 hours.

2 tablespoons olive oil

1 tablespoon ground coriander

½ teaspoon hot chilli powder

1 teaspoon ground turmeric

1 teaspoon ground cinnamon

6 green cardamoms, crushed

2 garlic cloves, finely chopped

2 medium onions, chopped

1 tablespoon finely chopped fresh ginger

700g roughly diced lamb, most fat removed

125ml boiling water

1 x 10g gluten-free chicken stock cube

salt and freshly ground black pepper

6 tablespoons double cream

2 tomatoes, roughly chopped

2 tablespoons fresh coriander, chopped

steamed basmati rice, to serve

Place the slow cooker pot on the stove, add the oil and warm gently.

Add the spices and cook gently for 2-3 minutes, to release their flavour, but do not burn.

Add the garlic, onions and ginger and cook over a low heat for 3-4 minutes to coat well in the spices and oil. Next add the lamb, water and crumbled stock cube, season well with salt and pepper, then place in the preheated slow cooker cradle set to low.

Cover and cook for 4-6 hours over a low heat.

Once cooked, the meat will be very tender. Skim off any surplus oil, stir well, then add the cream, tomatoes and coriander.

Check the seasoning and serve with steamed basmati rice.

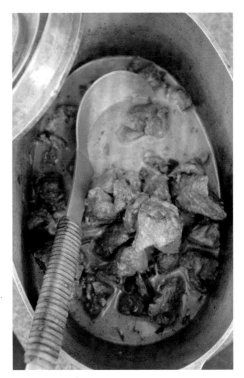

POT ROAST CHICKEN WITH SWEET BABY ONIONS

SERVES: 4-6
PREPARATION: 20mins
COOKING: 1 hour 20mins

Pot roasting is part roasting and part braising - the meat is slowly cooked in a covered dish. I like to roast chicken with a little wine and plenty of big flavours such as lemon and thyme. The braised vinegar onions make a deliciously different accompaniment to the tender chicken.

1 x 1.25kg fresh chicken

1 large lemon, halved

600g baby onions or shallots, peeled but with the root left on

1 small bunch fresh thyme

125ml dry white wine

1 x 10g gluten-free chicken stock cube

3 tablespoons balsamic vinegar

2 teaspoons caster sugar

100g unsalted butter, cubed

2 tablespoons cornflour

4 tablespoons water

salt and freshly ground black pepper

mashed potato, to serve

Preheat the oven to 180°C/350°F/gas mark 4.

Put the lemon halves inside the chicken. Place the chicken in a large flameproof casserole dish.

Place the onions around the bird, along with the thyme, wine, crumbled stock cube, vinegar, sugar, butter and seasoning.

Place the dish over a low heat and bring to a simmer. Once the liquid starts to bubble place the lid on top and pop into the oven for 1 hour.

Once cooked, remove the chicken and thyme stalks from the pan.

Gently cook down the onions and stock for 10 minutes on the hob or until it forms a gravy-like consistency.

Mix the cornflour and water together in a cup to form a smooth paste. Stir the paste into the simmering mixture, stirring all the time and the juices will thicken nicely. Serve the chicken whole or jointed on a large plate with the onion stew alongside. I love mash with this dish.

LEMON AND LEEK RISOTTO

Risottos are very popular at the moment, and I really like them – they make a complete meal in one bowl. You can add almost anything to a risotto and it will taste good. The secret is to not overcook the rice, and to keep it nice and soupy. Any leftover rice can be made into arancini (see page 131).

6 tablespoons olive oil

1 small onion, finely chopped

2 garlic cloves, finely chopped

1 small leek, very finely shredded

300g arborio rice

100ml white wine

1 x 10g gluten-free vegetable stock cube

600ml boiling water

150g Parmesan cheese, grated

2 tablespoons chopped fresh basil

zest of 1 lemon, shredded into long pieces

25g unsalted butter

salt and freshly ground black pepper

grated Parmesan cheese, to serve

Heat 2 tablespoons of the olive oil in a small, shallow pan, add the onion and garlic and cook for 10 minutes to soften.

Heat the remaining oil in a separate medium-size pan, and add the leek. Season well with salt and pepper. Cook for 4-5 minutes, stirring all the time, until cooked, but not overcooked. Then pop into a colander to drain well.

Add the rice to the shallow pan and coat well in the oil, then add the white wine and reduce until almost evaporated.

Crumble the stock cube over the rice, and then gradually add the boiling water a little at a time, stirring constantly. Add enough water until the rice is cooked (12–15 minutes), not overcooked: nice and soupy. Taste the rice (there should be a little resistance between the teeth when tasted) and season well.

Once you are happy with the base, add the cheese, cooked leek, lemon zest, basil and butter. Cover and leave for 5 minutes.

Check the consistency (it should be like thick soup), and add a little boiling water if it seems too thick. Serve in deep bowls with extra Parmesan cheese.

SALADS, DRESSINGS & QUICK FIXES

MINTED PEA FUSILLI SALAD WITH MOZZARELLA

Peas make a good soup and they're also great for sauces and salad dressings. This idea is a quick-fire recipe that is very fresh, easy to prepare and really different. Any cubed cheese can be used but do not add it to the dish until the last second, so it does not melt too much in the sauce. The lemon juice really lifts the dish, but sprinkle it over just before serving or the brilliant green colour will fade.

500g gluten-free fusilli pasta

250g frozen peas

2 tablespoons olive oil

1 tablespoon gluten-free Dijon mustard

150-200ml strong vegetable stock*

3 tablespoons chopped fresh sage

1 small radicchio lettuce, finely shredded

50g baby spinach leaves

salt and cracked black pepper

300g mozzarella, cut into small cubes

juice of ½ lemon

Cook the pasta in boiling water until just tender, then drain and keep warm.

Cook the peas in plenty of boiling salted water for 1-2 minutes; drain well.

Pop half the peas into a liquidiser or food processor with the olive oil and mustard and blitz. Gradually add enough vegetable stock to give you a nice, thick green purée.

Add the sage to the warm pasta along with the radicchio, spinach and the remaining whole peas, then stir in the warm pea sauce. Season and stir well.

Top with the diced mozzarella, squeeze over the lemon juice and sprinkle with cracked black pepper and serve immediately.

* Make the stock up using half the amount of water specified on the pack instructions.

SWEET AND SOUR AUBERGINE SALAD WITH ALMOND PESTO

SERVES: 4
PREPARATION: 20mins
COOKING: 25-30mins

I find aubergines a bit dull really; they only ever really taste of what you put with them. But handled correctly, they are delicious. Here is a classic example, where they are combined with sweet and sour flavours, chilli, almonds and basil. One tip: always slightly overcook the aubergines as they will taste much nicer.

For the roasted vegetables

12 cooked small new potatoes, halved

1 large aubergine, diced into 1cm cubes

4 tablespoons olive oil

½ teaspoon salt

½ teaspoon coarsely ground black pepper

2 teaspoons brown sugar

2 tablespoons tamarind paste

For the pesto

2 garlic cloves, finely chopped

20 fresh basil leaves

50g whole unskinned almonds, lightly toasted

6-8 tablespoons olive oil

1 tablespoon finely grated Pecorino cheese, finely grated

For the salad

200g mozzarella, diced into 1cm cubes

100g mixed salad leaves

200g cooked fine green beans, sliced diagonally in half

12 cherry tomatoes, halved

2 tablespoons sultanas

1 teaspoon fresh finely chopped red chilli

salt and ground black pepper

Preheat the oven to 220°C/425°F/gas mark 7.

Place the cooked potatoes and aubergine in a roasting tin, add the oil and stir well. Next, add the salt, pepper, sugar and tamarind paste and mix really well. Cook for 25-30 minutes, or until very soft and cooked – slightly overcooked is better for this salad.

Place all the pesto ingredients in a food processor and blend until fairly smooth, adding a little more oil if needed to get a smooth consistency.

Mix the roasted salad ingredients together in bowl, then add the mozzarella and mixed leaves, but do not overwork. Finally add the beans, tomatoes, sultanas and chilli and season well with salt and pepper. Mix together gently and divide between 4 plates. Spoon over the pesto to serve.

ROASTED BEETROOT, ORANGE AND ROCKET SALAD

I just love roasted beetroots – they're packed with flavour. The secret is to not cut off the root, as they will bleed out their colour during cooking. Also, trim the stalks close to the crown but don't cut into the bulb itself. There are many varieties of beetroots available these days, ranging from red ringed to white; my favourite variety is called Yellow Burpee and has an orangey-red skin and yellow flesh.

The top parts of the leaves and stalks, especially from young beets, make a lovely salad accompaniment, but do wash them thoroughly.

6 medium beetroots, thoroughly washed

1 large orange

2 tablespoons cider vinegar

150g thick natural yogurt

2 tablespoons clear honey

2 small shallots, finely sliced

2 heads Belgian chicory, finely sliced on the angle

50g fresh rocket

a few beetroot leaves, thoroughly washed

salt and freshly ground black pepper

Preheat the oven to 200°C/400°F/gas mark 6. Wrap the beetroots in foil and place on a baking tray.

Cook the beetroots for 45 minutes to an hour, or until a knife passes through them easily. Finely grate the zest from the orange, and place in a bowl. Add the cider vinegar, season and mix well. Next, peel the orange and remove the segments, squeezing the juice from them into a separate bowl.

Once the beetroots are cooked, remove from the oven and leave to cool for 15 minutes. Unwrap the cooled beetroot and the skin will rub off easily, due to the steam produced by the cooking process. Trim off the beetroot stalks and tails, then cut each beetroot into 5-6 wedges and pop them into the orange zest mixture; mix well.

Combine the yogurt, honey and a shake of salt and pepper and stir in the orange juice. Spoon the yogurt mixture over the beetroots, then add the shallots and the chicory and mix well. Add the rocket and beetroot leaves and mix lightly. Do not overwork or the salad will collapse. Serve straight away.

QUINOA BASMATI RICE AND SALTED CASHEW SALAD

SERVES: 4
PREPARATION: 10mins
COOKING: 15-20mins

I like to eat this lovely nutty salad on its own, warm, with a poached egg on top.

150g quinoa

200g cooked basmati rice, still warm

100g rocket, roughly chopped

100g watercress, roughly chopped

100g salted honeyed cashews, chopped

5 tablespoons extra virgin olive oil

juice of 2 large limes

juice of 1 orange

1 garlic clove, crushed

1 large red onion, finely sliced

Place the quinoa in a pan, cover with cold water and bring to a gentle simmer. Cook for 15-20 minutes until nice and nutty, then strain well and add the warmed rice. Tip into a large salad bowl and stir in the rocket, watercress and cashews.

Place the oil, lime and orange juices in a small bowl, then add the garlic and red onion and mix well. Pour the dressing over the rice and quinoa salad, mix well again and serve.

HOT AND SOUR RED CABBAGE AND PAPAYA SALAD

SERVES: 4
PREPARATION: 25mins
plus at least 2 hours
marinating time
COOKING: none

I love the sour and sweet taste combinations here. If you can leave the salad overnight, all the better – the veg will soften nicely and the flavours will intensify.

½ small red cabbage, very finely sliced

2 large red onions, finely sliced

50g fresh ginger, very finely chopped

1 small red chilli, finely chopped

100g young runner or flat beans, finely cut on the diagonal

finely grated zest and juice of 4 large limes

2 tablespoons palm or soft brown sugar

2 tablespoons tamarind paste (check it is a gluten-free variety)

8 tablespoons sunflower oil

1 papaya, deseeded and sliced into long strips

4 tablespoons chopped fresh basil

salt and freshly ground black pepper

Place the cabbage, onions, ginger, chilli and beans together in a bowl and mix really well. In a separate bowl, whisk together the lime zest and juice, sugar, tamarind paste, oil and salt and pepper. Pour the dressing over the salad, and stir thoroughly to combine. Cover and leave to marinate for at least 2 hours or overnight if possible. Once marinated, give the salad a good stir, then add the papaya and fresh basil and mix well. Serve with poached chicken, grilled fish or a couple of soft-boiled eggs.

HAZELNUT AND ARTICHOKE SALAD WITH SHERRY VINEGAR

SERVES: 4
PREPARATION: 15mins
COOKING: none

A simple, easy salad made from store-cupboard ingredients; nevertheless, very nice to eat.

2 x 285g jars artichokes, well drained
100g roasted hazelnuts, roughly chopped
100g firm goat's cheese, cut into 1cm cubes
4 tablespoons olive oil

juice of ½ lemon
2 tablespoons sherry vinegar
½ iceberg lettuce, finely sliced
salt and freshly ground black pepper

Place the artichokes, hazelnuts and goat's cheese in a large serving bowl and mix well. Add the olive oil, lemon juice and vinegar and again mix really well. Season with salt and pepper, then stir in the lettuce just before serving.

SPINACH, FETA AND STRAWBERRY SALAD

SERVES: 4
PREPARATION: 15mins
COOKING: none

This, to me, is a perfectly balanced salad. I find the stronger the cheese the better and feta is perfect with its acidic edge. Likewise, Lancashire is also a good companion.

100g baby spinach leaves
½ small red onion, very finely sliced
80g feta cheese, cubed
8 ripe but not soft strawberries, quartered
2 tablespoons lightly toasted pine nuts

For the dressing
2 teaspoons Dijon mustard (check it is gluten-free)
4 tablespoons balsamic vinegar
salt and freshly cracked black pepper
8 tablespoons extra virgin olive oil

First make the dressing. Place the mustard, vinegar, salt and pepper in a bowl. Whisk for 20 seconds, then gradually add the oil, whisking continuously to emulsify nicely.

Place the spinach, onion and cheese in a large bowl and toss together. Add the strawberries and fold in gently so they do not break up. Spoon over half the dressing, season lightly and gently mix again.

Divide the salad between four serving plates, sprinkle over the nuts and serve extra vinaigrette on the side. (For the best flavour, everything must be at room temperature.)

SIMPLE CHICORY, FIG AND ORANGE SALAD

To me, when it comes to cooking, less is more. And this recipe is a perfect example of those carefully chosen words and a truly great combination. If figs are not available, then a poached pear cut into six is a good alternative. This salad is best prepared just before you want to serve it.

2 large oranges
75ml orange juice
40ml extra virgin olive oil
1 teaspoon red wine vinegar
30g gluten-free Dijon mustard
2 little gem lettuces, halved

2 heads chicory
75g rocket or baby spinach leaves
60g Parmesan cheese, finely sliced using a
    potato peeler
4 ripe figs, sliced into 6
salt, sugar and freshly ground black pepper, to taste

Finely grate the zest from one of the oranges. Peel and segment both the oranges, so that you have 12-14 segments set aside.

Make the dressing by whisking together the orange zest, orange juice, oil, vinegar and mustard. Add salt and sugar to taste.

Divide the lettuce between 4 deep bowls.

Finely slice the chicory on the diagonal, then divide between the dishes. The chicory will discolour quickly; that's quite normal.

Sprinkle over the rocket or spinach leaves. Top each bowl with one quarter of the Parmesan slices, orange segments and fig slices.

Drizzle over 3 tablespoons of the dressing, a dusting of black pepper and serve straight away.

SWEET AND SOUR TAMARIND PICKLED CUCUMBER SALAD

SERVES: 4
PREPARATION: 50mins plus freezing and 30mins soaking
COOKING: 10-15mins

A nice, fresh-tasting salad, which goes well with all lightly cooked fish or steamed or poached chicken. The key here is to freeze the cucumbers solid first, then defrost, pat dry and slice into thin strips. The freezing process makes the strips of cucumber really pliable, also giving them a beautiful translucent quality.

2 large cucumbers

25g kombu seaweed (optional)

4 tablespoons rice wine vinegar

3 tablespoons tamarind paste

2 tablespoons mirin

3 tablespoons tamari or gluten-free soy sauce

1 tablespoon caster sugar

2 tablespoons olive oil

1 tablespoon black onion seeds

1 tablespoon chopped pickled ginger

salt and freshly ground black pepper

Place the whole cucumbers in the freezer until solid. Then allow them to defrost. Soak the kombu in cold water for 30 minutes.

Pat the cucumbers dry and slice into thin strips. Sprinkle 1 teaspoon of salt over the strips, mix well and leave to drain for 20 minutes. This toughens up the strips and removes a little more juice.

Meanwhile, place the soaked seaweed in a saucepan, bring to the boil, then simmer until soft but still slightly chewy. Drain well and slice into very thin strips.

Rinse the salt off the cucumber, and pat dry again, then mix with the seaweed. In a separate bowl, mix the remaining ingredients together to make the dressing, season, then pour over the cucumber and seaweed. Mix well.

Leave for 20 minutes, then serve - it's as easy as that!

CHORIZO, RED ONION AND BUTTER BEAN SALAD

SERVES: 4-6
PREPARATION: 15mins
COOKING: 10mins

A very simple, colourful and tasty salad. When the chorizo is cooked it releases a wonderful orangey-red oil that adds a fantastic flavour to the finished dish.

For the salad

250g chorizo sausage

2 tablespoons olive oil

1 large red onion, cut into thin wedges, root intact

4 tablespoons roughly chopped fresh parsley

2 x 425g tins butter beans, drained

20 cherry tomatoes, halved

For the dressing

2 garlic cloves, crushed

1 tablespoon lemon juice

5 tablespoons sherry vinegar

8 tablespoons extra virgin olive oil

salt and freshly ground black pepper

rice crackers or Parmesan Spoon Bread (see recipe on page 44), to serve

Preheat a large frying pan, add the chorizo and cook gently for 2-3 minutes to release the natural oils. Brown slightly, then remove and keep warm.

Next add the olive oil to the pan and cook the onion wedges until slightly softened, the onions will be coated in the lovely chorizo oil.

Meanwhile, place the parsley, beans and tomatoes in a large bowl, then add the hot onions and chorizo and mix well.

Combine the garlic, lemon juice, vinegar, oil and finally a little salt and pepper and mix well. Serve in deep bowls with rice crackers or Parmesan Spoon Bread for a simple and very tasty light lunch or supper.

SERVES: 4
PREPARATION: 10mins
COOKING: 15mins

WARM TUNA, CAULIFLOWER AND PAPRIKA SALAD

This combination of salad ingredients sounds odd I know, but it really does work - light, packed full of flavour and a really nice accompaniment to lightly seared tuna. I prefer to use fresh skipjack tuna, as it is very common and not in danger of over-fishing. In fact, it's sometimes known as 'the rat of the sea', as it is so plentiful!

For the salad

4 tablespoons olive oil

1 large onion, finely chopped

½ teaspoon smoked paprika

300g cauliflower florets

125ml dry white wine

30g pine nuts, toasted

65g raisins, soaked

salt and ground white pepper

For the tuna

2 teaspoons vegetable oil

4 x 120g tuna steaks

pinch of cracked black pepper

basmati rice, steamed green beans and lime wedges, to serve

Heat the oil in a saucepan, add the onion and paprika and cook for 5 minutes.

Stir in the cauliflower and white wine, season well with salt and white pepper, then cover with a tight-fitting lid. Turn down the heat and cook for about 5 minutes or until the cauliflower is just cooked, but not overcooked.

Remove the lid and add the pine nuts and raisins and mix well.

To cook the tuna, heat the oil in a frying pan or griddle over a medium heat. Sprinkle the steaks with cracked black pepper, then sear well on both sides in the preheated pan; this should take no longer than 20-30 seconds on each side - keep the tuna very pink.

Spoon the cauliflower and raisins around the edge of each plate, spoon some basmati rice into the centre and sprinkle over a few green beans. Top with the tuna and serve with lime wedges.

FRESH MUSSEL VINAIGRETTE WITH RED ONIONS AND PLUM TOMATOES

SERVES: 4
PREPARATION: 15mins
COOKING: 10mins

As a child, I remember my father consuming large amounts of all sorts of shellfish. His favourite was whelks with lots of vinegar, salt and black pepper. I also love all shellfish and this dish is a twist on my childhood memories, only updated with red onions and fresh ripe tomatoes.

200ml gluten-free fish stock

100ml dry white wine

1kg fresh mussels, scrubbed and bearded

4 tablespoons olive oil

1 small red onion, very finely sliced

1 small red pepper, diced into small cubes

2 garlic cloves, finely chopped

6 large, fresh, ripe plum tomatoes, chopped into 1cm dice

2 tablespoons chopped fresh flat-leaf parsley

2 tablespoons red wine vinegar

salt and freshly ground white pepper

Bring the stock and white wine to the boil in a large pan, add the mussels and cover.

Cook the mussels for 6–8 minutes, stirring occasionally. Do not overcook or the mussels will become tough. Discard any unopened ones.

Place the mussels in a colander, and carefully remove all the flesh from the shells, checking there are no bits of gristle or sand particles.

Heat the oil in a frying pan and add the onion, pepper and garlic and soften slightly, about 3-4 minutes. Place in a serving bowl; add the mussels, tomatoes, parsley and vinegar, then season to taste. Mix well, but carefully. Adjust the seasoning if needed and serve either straight away or well chilled.

SUNBLUSH TOMATO BASIL DRESSING

Sunblush tomatoes are all the rage at the moment and they are very versatile. I particularly like them in a punchy dressing with wholegrain mustard.

2 teaspoons gluten-free wholegrain mustard

2 tablespoons white wine vinegar

250ml rapeseed oil

200g sunblush tomatoes, roughly chopped

2 bunches fresh basil, roughly chopped

salt and freshly ground black pepper

Place the mustard and vinegar in a small, deep bowl. Season and whisk well. Gradually add the oil in a thin stream, whisking well. Finally, stir in the chopped sunblush tomatoes and basil just before serving.

HONEY AND MUSTARD SALAD DRESSING

SERVES: approx 250ml
PREPARATION: 5mins
COOKING: none

This has to be one of my favourite dressings – its clean, simple flavours work well not only with salad but with meat and vegetables too.

1 tablespoon gluten-free Dijon mustard

1 teaspoon gluten-free wholegrain mustard

1 tablespoon clear honey

4 tablespoons cider vinegar

150ml good olive oil

salt and freshly ground black pepper

Combine the mustards, honey, vinegar and seasoning together. Whisk in the olive oil, to make a nice thick dressing. Taste and add a little more vinegar or honey, as you like it. Cover securely, store in the refrigerator and serve at room temperature.

SERVES: 4
PREPARATION: 10mins
COOKING: none

CITRUS DRESSING

Citrus dressings are very nice with crunchy lettuces, raw vegetables and fish. This dressing is quite tart, so you could add sugar if you wanted. Alternatively, you could reduce the orange and add grapefruit or lime juice for a more astringent dressing.

1 heaped tablespoon gluten-free wholegrain mustard

150ml fresh orange juice

50ml extra virgin olive oil

3 tablespoons chopped fresh basil

3 tablespoons chopped fresh dill

3 tablespoons chopped fresh parsley

salt and freshly ground black pepper

Place the mustard and orange juice in a small deep bowl. Season and whisk well. Gradually add the oil in a thin stream, whisking well.

Finally, stir in the herbs 5 minutes before serving, this ensures they keep their brilliant green colour.

SPICY YOGURT AND MAPLE DRESSING

Quite a different dressing, great for drizzling over roasted pork or steamed chicken; also good on crunchy lettuces such as iceberg or romaine.

2 teaspoons gluten-free Dijon mustard

2 garlic cloves, crushed

2 tablespoons white wine vinegar

3 tablespoons maple syrup

pinch of dried red chilli seeds

100ml extra virgin olive oil

175g natural yogurt

juice of ½ lemon

salt and freshly ground black pepper

Place the mustard, garlic, vinegar, maple syrup and chilli seeds in a small deep bowl, season and whisk well. Gradually add the oil in a thin stream, whisking well. Finally add the yogurt and lemon juice and whisk well again. Check the seasoning and the consistency – it should be like thick cream. Adjust with a little cold water if it is too thick.

GARLIC AND CORIANDER DRESSING

This dressing works well with poached or steamed fish, and of course vegetable salads.

1 tablespoon gluten-free Dijon mustard

3 tablespoons white wine vinegar

1 garlic clove, finely chopped

6 tablespoons extra virgin olive oil

4 tablespoons chopped fresh coriander

salt and freshly ground black pepper

Place the mustard, vinegar and garlic in a small deep bowl. Season and whisk well. Add a dash of water and whisk again, then gradually add the oil in a thin stream, whisking well. The dressing will thicken nicely due to the mustard emulsifying the oil and water. You may need to add a little more water to thin the dressing slightly. Finally, taste and adjust the seasoning if needed. Stir in the coriander 5 minutes before serving, to ensure it keeps its brilliant green colour.

BASIC FRENCH DRESSING

SERVES: 4
PREPARATION: 10mins
COOKING: none

Great for simple leaf salad and tomatoes but also nice with warm potato salad or freshly boiled new potatoes. I like to add a little shallot to give it a bit of a kick.

2 teaspoons gluten-free Dijon mustard

2 teaspoons white wine vinegar

6 tablespoons rapeseed oil

2 shallots, very finely chopped

salt and freshly ground black pepper

Place the mustard and vinegar in a small deep bowl. Season and whisk well. Gradually add the oil in a thin stream, whisking well. Stir in the shallots.

The dressing may emulsify or it may not – it's no real problem, I like a split dressing. Stir well just before serving.

CHESTNUT, GOAT'S CHEESE AND PARSLEY PESTO

SERVES: 4
PREPARATION: 10mins
COOKING: none

I think this combination of flavours works really well. Try it with cooked flat gluten-free pasta such as tagliatelle or with any cooked meat or fish.

60g spinach

60g goat's cheese (the harder the better)

50g Parmesan cheese

4 tablespoons chopped fresh basil

50g vacuum-packed cooked chestnuts

30g pine nuts

½ teaspoon sugar

4 tablespoons olive oil

squeeze of lemon juice, to taste

salt and freshly ground black pepper

Place the spinach, cheeses, basil, chestnuts, pine nuts, sugar and a little salt and pepper in a food processor. Blitz, then add the oil in a thin stream until you have a thickish sauce. You may need to add a little more or less oil to get the desired consistency. Spoon into a bowl, adjust the seasoning and add the lemon juice to taste.

SERVES: 4
PREPARATION: 10mins
plus 30mins chilling
COOKING: none

CHERRY TOMATO AND AVOCADO SALSA

I love the simplicity of this really tasty dish. It works well with gluten-free crackers, gluten-free pasta or over grilled chicken or fish.

½ small onion, finely chopped

1 small red chilli, deseeded and finely chopped

2 garlic cloves, chopped

2 teaspoons caster sugar

1 ripe avocado, diced into small cubes

2 tablespoons sherry vinegar

15 cherry tomatoes, quartered

3 tablespoons chopped fresh coriander

salt and freshly ground black pepper

Mix together the onion, chilli, garlic and sugar, season well with salt and pepper. Add the avocado, vinegar, tomatoes and coriander and mix well. Chill for 30 minutes, stirring occasionally. Taste and re-season, if necessary, before serving.

SERVES: 4-6
PREPARATION: 20mins
COOKING: 30mins

ROAST PUMPKIN, SWEET CHILLI AND ROCKET TAPENADE

I love the flavour and beautiful colour of this tapenade. It's delicious on toast, as a dip or as a stir-through sauce for gluten-free pasta or rice.

400g pumpkin or squash, cut into small chunks

1 red onion, finely sliced

3 garlic cloves

8 tablespoons olive oil

3 tablespoons balsamic vinegar

2 teaspoons caster sugar

¼ teaspoon dried chilli flakes

50g rocket

salt and freshly ground black pepper

Preheat the oven to 220ºC/425ºF/gas mark 7. Place the pumpkin or squash, onion, garlic, 4 tablespoons of the oil, vinegar, sugar and chilli flakes together in a bowl and mix well. Season well with salt and pepper. Place the mixture on a large baking tray. Cook for 25-30 minutes until the mixture is well browned and the vegetables are cooked through. Carefully place the mixture in a food processor. Add the rocket and remaining oil, then process until you have a chunky purée. Spoon into a bowl, check the seasoning and adjust if needed. Serve hot or well chilled.

SWEET TOMATO SUMMER DIP

SERVES: 4-6
PREPARATION: 10mins
COOKING: 25-30mins

I really enjoy this sort of dip with a glass or two of white wine. It's very easy to prepare and cook, and will keep for up to a week in the fridge. It can also be used to accompany burgers or roasted, grilled or pan-fried fish. It makes a good barbecue dip as well.

4 tablespoons olive oil

1 medium onion, finely chopped

2 garlic cloves, roughly chopped

200g sunblush tomatoes, finely cubed

4 large vine tomatoes, roughly chopped

200ml tomato juice

2 tablespoons muscovado sugar

½ x 10g gluten-free stock cube

2 tablespoons cornflour

50g pine nuts, lightly toasted

4 tablespoons roughly chopped fresh basil

1-2 tablespoons extra virgin olive oil

salt and freshly ground black pepper

Heat the olive oil in a medium pan, add the onion and garlic and cook for 5-6 minutes to soften slightly. Next, add the sunblush and vine tomatoes, tomato juice, sugar, crumbled stock cube and 200ml water; season and cook down gently until you have a thickish stew.

In a cup or small bowl, mix the cornflour with 2 tablespoons cold water, then stir into the stew and bring to the boil, stirring constantly, so it will thicken nicely. Once this is done, remove from the heat and leave to cool.

Check the seasoning; adjust if needed, then stir in the pine nuts, fresh basil and enough extra virgin olive oil to moisten nicely. That's it! Serve with rice crackers and a nice glass of chilled, dry white wine.

GRILLED ASPARAGUS WITH OLIVE MASH

English asparagus, to me, is the best in the world. The flavour is so delicious it's perfect eaten as it is. The only problem is, the English asparagus season is short and it usually only lasts through May and June. So make the most of it!

For the mash

450g potatoes

150ml warm milk

75g unsalted butter, melted

pinch of ground nutmeg

20 pitted black olives, roughly chopped

2 tablespoons roughly chopped fresh chives

salt and freshly ground black pepper

For the dressing

½ small onion, finely chopped

1 teaspoon gluten-free Dijon mustard

3 tablespoons balsamic vinegar

5 tablespoons sunflower oil

For the asparagus

20 young English asparagus spears

2 tablespoons olive oil

Boil the potatoes in salted water until tender. Drain and mash with the milk and butter and stir well. Finally, add the nutmeg, chopped olives and chives and mix well. You may need to add a little more milk to get a smooth, but not runny, mash. Cover the pan until ready to serve – the mash will keep warm in the pan.

Next, make the dressing. Place the onion in a small, deep bowl, add the mustard, vinegar and 2 tablespoons of cold water and stir well. Season with salt and pepper and stir well again so they dissolve. Gradually add the oil in a thin stream, whisking constantly. If the vinaigrette splits don't worry too much; just make sure you stir it well before serving.

Heat a griddle or frying pan, brush the asparagus spears with the olive oil and season well. Cook the asparagus in the hot pan for 2–3 minutes on each side, so they take on a nice colour and go slightly limp. You may have to cook the asparagus in a couple of batches.

To serve, spoon a blob of mash into the middle of a hot plate, lay 5 pieces of cooked asparagus over the mash and finally drizzle over a little dressing. Don't go overboard with the dressing – it's very powerful! A nice glass of chilled Sauvignon Blanc is the perfect accompaniment.

SERVES: 4-6
PREPARATION: 10mins
COOKING: none

FRESH CORIANDER PESTO

This is quite unusual and Italian purists may be up in arms, but I think it's great! Take care though, as the lemon juice acid will react with the brilliant green of the coriander and discolour it slightly, so add it at the last moment. Serve the pesto with gluten-free pasta, rice, roasted vegetables or simply as a dip.

50g pine nuts
2 small shallots, finely chopped
2 garlic cloves, finely chopped
70g fresh coriander
30g Parmesan cheese, grated

pinch of red chilli flakes
80ml sunflower oil
salt and freshly ground black pepper
½ lemon, to serve

Preheat the oven to 200°C/400°F/gas mark 6. Place the pine nuts on a baking tray and roast until lightly browned, but not burnt. This will intensify their flavour. Set aside to cool.

Place the shallots, garlic, coriander, Parmesan, chilli, ½ teaspoon of freshly ground black pepper and salt in a food processor. Add half the oil and blitz until fairly smooth.

Gradually add the remaining oil until you have the desired consistency.

Spoon into a bowl and season to taste. Add a squeeze or two of lemon juice to bring out the flavour just before serving.

ROASTED LEMON AND GARLIC PESTO

SERVES: 4-6
PREPARATION: 20mins
COOKING: 20mins

I love this recipe – it was developed by a good friend of mine, Steven Poole, after a trip to Sicily. Yes, it's unusual, but its unique taste works well with roasted white meats, chicken and grilled or barbecued fish such as swordfish, red or grey mullet and mackerel.

2 large lemons, cut roughly into 8 pieces each

½ very small onion, finely chopped

7 tablespoons olive oil (approximately)

¼ teaspoon salt

¼ teaspoon cracked black pepper

2 tablespoons caster sugar

75g roasted hazelnuts

2 garlic cloves

4 tablespoons chopped fresh basil

2-3 tablespoons lemon juice

50g Parmesan cheese, grated

1 tablespoon sugar

salt and freshly ground black pepper

Preheat the oven to 220°C/425°F/gas mark 7.

In a large bowl mix the lemons, onion, 2 tablespoons olive oil, ¼ teaspoon salt, ¼ teaspoon cracked pepper and 1 tablespoon sugar.

Place on a non-stick baking tray and cook for 15-20 minutes, or until the lemon is browning slightly and nice and soft. Once cooked, leave to cool.

When cool, place the lemon mixture in a food processor, along with the hazelnuts, garlic, basil, lemon juice, cheese, remaining sugar and a good pinch or two of salt and pepper.

Process until fairly smooth and then add the remaining oil in a steady stream until the pesto is a spooning consistency. Spoon into a bowl, check the seasoning and adjust if needed.

Store in a sealed jar or container in the fridge for up to 10 days.

PARTIES & ENTERTAINING

THE RECIPES: ORGANIC CHICKEN AND PRAWN JAMBALAYA / GRILLED CHICKEN WITH HONEY-GLAZED FIGS / EASTER ROAST CHICKEN WITH TARRAGON AND ASPARAGUS / EASY GRILLED PHEASANT WITH BACON AND CHESTNUTS / BRINED, PAN-FRIED DUCK BREAST WITH ORANGES / CAJUN SPICED SALMON WITH HONEY CRÈME FRAÎCHE / MARINATED MACKEREL WITH WARM POTATO SALAD/ BAKED RED MULLET WITH MUSHROOMS AND LEMON / TWICE BAKED PORK WITH SWEET POTATO AND RED ONION STIR-FRY / GRILLED RUMP STEAK WITH RED WINE BUTTER / CHEDDAR, BACON, ROASTED PUMPKIN AND RED PEPPER DIP / PIL PIL PRAWNS / SALT AND PEPPER DEEP-FRIED SQUID WITH CHERMOULA / INDIAN-STYLE POPCORN / FRESH PEA HOUMOUS / DEEP FRIED ARANCINI WITH CHICKPEA DIP / SMOKED DUCK ROLLS WITH SWEET RELISH / GLUTEN-FREE PIZZA BASE / POLENTA-CRUSTED PARSLEY ONION RINGS / WASABI CUCUMBER SHRIMP CRACKERS

ORGANIC CHICKEN AND PRAWN JAMBALAYA

This is basically a pilaf with a trendy name, although I have to say it's one of my favourites. Originally from the States, it hasn't really caught on in Europe, but the mix of rice, chicken and shellfish is not a new idea – the Spanish have their paella and the Indians have biryani.

2 tablespoons olive oil

1 medium onion, finely chopped

1 garlic clove, crushed

1 red pepper, cut into 1cm strips

2 celery sticks, cut into 1cm pieces

1 large chicken breast, skinned and cut into 2cm pieces

2 teaspoons smoked paprika

1 bay leaf

600ml strong chicken stock*

2 gluten-free spicy sausages (chorizo are perfect), cut into 2cm chunks

2 teaspoons tomato purée

160g long-grain rice

6 spring onions, finely chopped

180g peeled prawns

salt and freshly ground black pepper

Preheat the oven to 200°C/400°F/gas mark 6.

Heat the olive oil in a large flameproof casserole dish. Add the onion, garlic, pepper, celery and cook for 5 minutes over a high heat to colour.

Add the chicken, paprika and bay leaf, and cook until the chicken turns opaque on the outside. Meanwhile bring the chicken stock to the boil in a small pan.

Next, add the sausage, tomato purée and rice and cover with the boiling stock. Stir well, season and bring to the boil. Cover and cook in the oven for 15-18 minutes or until all the stock is absorbed.

Remove the lid from the dish, add the spring onions and prawns, re-season and leave to stand for 5 minutes. Serve hot and piled high in bowls.

* Make the stock up using half the amount of water specified on the pack instructions.

GRILLED CHICKEN WITH HONEY-GLAZED FIGS

SERVES: 4
PREPARATION: 15mins plus at least 2 hours marinating
COOKING: 20mins

There is something so nice about warm grilled figs and chicken, they just seem to go together really well. The ripe figs will start to burst when they are grilled, so the secret is to warm them through very gently rather than cook them.

4 medium chicken breasts, skin on

2 tablespoons gluten-free Worcestershire sauce

dash or 2 of Tabasco sauce

juice of 2 large lemons

8 fresh, ripe figs

2 tablespoons clear honey

2 tablespoons sherry vinegar

salt and freshly ground black pepper

green salad, to serve

Using a sharp knife, score the chicken skin in a criss-cross pattern.

Place the Worcestershire sauce, Tabasco sauce and lemon juice in a shallow dish, season and mix well. Place the chicken breasts in the dish and thoroughly coat in the mixture. Leave to marinate for at least 2 hours or overnight if possible.

Cut the figs in half lengthways, then cut each half into 3 or 4 wedges, making sure you do not cut all the way through, so you end up with a concertina effect. Drizzle the honey and vinegar over the cut figs and leave to marinate for 20 minutes.

Preheat the grill to high. Pop the chicken breasts onto a tray or dish then place under the grill and cook for 6-7 minutes on each side. Once cooked, remove and cover with foil. Meanwhile, place the figs in a baking dish or tray and grill them to just warm through; do not overcook or you will not be able to lift them.

Slice the chicken breast into 3-4 slices and arrange on 4 plates. Place 4 halves of cooked figs on each plate. All you need then is a large glass of Sauvignon Blanc and a green salad to make a perfect lunch!

SERVES: 6-8
PREPARATION: 15mins plus at least 4-5 hours chilling time
COOKING: none

SMOKED SALMON MOUSSE WITH AVOCADO AND DILL

This is a very simple mousse with very good end results. If you can make it a day in advance, so much the better.

250g smoked salmon off-cuts

4 tablespoons finely chopped fresh parsley

2-3 tablespoons brandy

salt and freshly ground black pepper

200g cream cheese (check it is gluten-free)

a dash of milk

250-300g smoked salmon, cut into long slices

2 large avocadoes

4 tablespoons chopped fresh dill

1 tablespoon olive oil

juice of 1 large lemon

Place the salmon off-cuts, parsley, brandy and pepper in a food processer and blitz until fairly smooth, then scrape the sides of the bowl down well. Add the cream cheese and milk and blitz again, then taste and adjust the seasoning if necessary.

Take 6-8 small bowls or ramekins (or use one large bowl if you prefer) and line each one with clingfilm, then take the long smoked salmon strips and arrange them over the clingfilm to cover the sides of each dish. Spoon the mousse into the bowls and pack down until each one is nicely and tightly filled. Cover the base with the remaining salmon and cover again with clingfilm.

Place the mousses in the fridge for at least 4-5 hours, or preferably overnight.

When ready to serve, chop the avocado into small cubes and place in a bowl with the dill, oil and salt and pepper and stir to combine. Turn the mousses out onto small plates, add a spoonful of avocado and a squeeze of lemon and serve.

EASY GRILLED PHEASANT WITH BACON AND CHESTNUTS

SERVES: 4
PREPARATION: 25mins
COOKING: 30mins

Game is becoming increasingly popular, thank goodness. It's delicious and very good value for money. Many supermarkets stock game now – if you haven't tried pheasant before then give this recipe a go – it's simple and so tasty. I love it!

1 tablespoon olive oil

60g pancetta or bacon

1 medium onion, finely sliced

1 carrot, finely chopped

2 bay leaves

pinch of ground cinnamon

1 tablespoon tomato purée

1 teaspoon fresh thyme leaves

1 teaspoon crushed garlic

pinch of ground cloves

125ml strong chicken or game stock*

125ml medium white wine

80g vacuum-packed cooked chestnuts

1 tablespoon cornflour (optional)

4 young pheasant breasts

4 slices Serrano ham

50g unsalted butter

salt and ground white pepper

mashed potatoes and sautéed cabbage, to serve

Place the oil in a large pan, add the pancetta or bacon and cook for about 10 minutes until slightly crisp.

Add the onion, carrot, bay leaves, cinnamon, tomato purée, thyme, garlic, ground cloves, chicken stock and white wine. Season well and simmer gently for 20 minutes.

When the vegetables are cooked, add the chestnuts, warm through gently, be careful as the chestnuts will break up if overcooked, and then check the seasoning.

The sauce should be a nice silky consistency. If it is not thick enough, combine the cornflour with 3 tablespoons of cold water in a cup, then gradually stir the paste into the simmering sauce until it thickens slightly.

Wrap the pheasant breasts in the Serrano ham. Heat the butter in a frying pan and sauté the pheasant breasts gently for 5-6 minutes on each side. It's important not to overcook pheasant, leave it pink and allow it to rest for 5 minutes.

Place the cooked pheasant breasts in deep bowls with a little sauce around them. I like to serve them with mashed potatoes and a little sautéed cabbage.

* Make the stock up using half the amount of water specified on the pack instructions.

SERVES: 4
PREPARATION: 15mins plus 20 mins marinating
COOKING: 30-35mins

BRINED, PAN-FRIED DUCK BREAST WITH ORANGES

Lightly brining any meat really changes not only the flavour but also the texture. It is an osmotic process and, simply put, this means that the water is sucked out of the cells in the meat and replaced by the sugar and salt in the brine. It's the same process that turns pork into bacon and it really alters the flavour of the meat.

4 medium duck breasts, skin on, lightly scored

For the brine
60g sugar
30g salt

Sauce
2 large oranges

200ml fresh orange juice
25g caster sugar
50ml cider vinegar
300ml strong chicken stock*
1 tablespoon cornflour
salt and freshly ground black pepper
mashed potatoes and peas, to serve

First, make the brine. Place the sugar, salt and 600ml water in a saucepan. Heat slowly over a low heat, then bring to the boil. Once the sugar and salt have dissolved, set aside to cool.

Once cooled, pour the brine into a measuring jug and bring the total volume back to 600ml with cold water. Pour half the brine into a small dish. Place the duck breasts in the dish so that they are arranged nice and snug. Pour over the rest of the brine. Cover and leave for 20 minutes, no more.

Peel the zest off the oranges and cut it into very fine strips (you should have about 2 tablespoons of zest). Peel the oranges and divide into segments (you need 12).

Next, place the orange zest, orange juice, sugar, cider vinegar and stock in a saucepan. Bring to the boil, then simmer until the volume has reduced by about two thirds. At this point, taste – if you have a really nice balance of acidity and orangey sweetness then it's ready. Bear in mind, the longer you reduce the sauce, the deeper the flavour will be.

In a small bowl or cup mix the cornflour with 3 tablespoons cold water, then add a little of the paste at a time to the simmering sauce, stirring constantly, just to thicken it slightly. Do not over-thicken. Season well with salt and pepper.

When the duck breasts are ready, rinse them off well under cold water, then pat really dry with kitchen paper.

Heat a non-stick frying pan and place the duck breasts, scored sides down in the hot pan. The skin will crackle straight away, and the fat will start to come out of the skin. After 4-5 minutes, turn over, and continue to cook for a further 4-5 minutes.

Once cooked, remove from the pan, place on a warm plate and cover with foil. Leave for 10 minutes to rest; this will ensure a soft, moist texture to the beautifully pink breast.

To serve, slice the breasts on a slight angle, drain well on kitchen paper and place on 4 plates. Top each breast with 3 orange segments, and spoon over the sauce. Serve with mashed potatoes and a few peas – delicious!

* Make the stock up using half the amount of water specified on the pack instructions.

CAJUN SPICED SALMON WITH HONEY CRÈME FRAÎCHE

Some years ago, I was fortunate enough to make a film about fly fishing in the Everglades. We caught many fine salmon trout and the boat's captain then filleted and flash-fried them, Cajun-style, with a brilliant red spicy rub, in a small shack right on the marina. It was sensational, so with that in mind, here is my version!

For the dressing

200g crème fraîche

2 tablespoons chopped fresh mint

2 tablespoons white wine vinegar

½ teaspoon cracked black pepper

2 tablespoons clear honey

3 spring onions, finely sliced on a diagonal

100g watercress sprigs and smoked paprika (optional), to serve

For the rub

2 teaspoons dried thyme

2 tablespoons paprika

2 tablespoons sea salt

1 tablespoon ground black pepper

3 teaspoons cayenne powder

1 tablespoon dried onion powder

1 tablespoon dried garlic powder

1 teaspoon ground bay leaves or dried leaves crushed with a rolling pin

1 teaspoon fennel seeds, crushed with a rolling pin

For the fish

2 tablespoons olive oil

4 x 140g fillets trout or salmon, skin on

Place all the dressing ingredients in a jug and whisk thoroughly with a fork, then set aside.

Mix all the spice rub ingredients together or blitz in a spice grinder. I have a brand new coffee grinder that I use for spices only.

Heat the oil in a frying pan and dust the fillets all over with the rub.

Add the fillets, skin-side down, and cook for 3-4 minutes, then flip over, and cook for a further 2 minutes. Do not overcook: the flesh should be half-cooked but warmed through; the flakes of flesh should push apart when pressed with a finger. Remove from the pan whilst still slightly undercooked.

Arrange the watercress onto 4 plates. Place the warm salmon fillets on the watercress. Spoon over the dressing and dust with a little smoked paprika, if using, and serve.

CHESTNUT, SPINACH AND WILD RICE CAKES WITH SPICED PARSNIP BROTH

SERVES: 4 as a starter
PREPARATION: 20mins
COOKING: 45–50mins

I love wild rice for its wonderful nutty taste and texture and, coupled with chestnuts, it makes this a lovely hearty dish. The broth can be made with any root vegetable.

salt and freshly ground black pepper

200g spinach, washed very well

500g potatoes

2 small onions, finely chopped

2 garlic cloves, crushed

100g wild rice, soaked overnight

3 tablespoons extra virgin olive oil

100g peeled chestnuts, roughly chopped

2 medium eggs, beaten

150g gluten-free breadcrumbs

a few tablespoons of gluten-free flour mix

(see recipe on page 152)

4–5 tablespoons vegetable oil

For the broth

50g unsalted butter

1 small parsnip, finely chopped

½ small onion, finely chopped

1 tablespoon aubergine or lime pickle

200ml gluten-free vegetable stock

1 small potato, finely chopped

a pinch of sugar

Bring a saucepan of salted water to the boil and cook the spinach for 2 minutes, then strain and refresh under cold water, before squeezing out all the liquid. Place the potatoes in the same cooking water and simmer for 30 minutes until soft, then mash and set aside.

Heat a little oil in a non-stick frying pan and sauté the onions until soft, then add the garlic and cook, stirring, then set aside. Place the wild rice in a sieve and rinse well under cold running water, then transfer to a clean pan, cover with water and bring to a rapid boil. Add 2 pinches of salt and cook until very soft, about 10 minutes. Strain and keep warm.

In a bowl, mix together the potato, rice, olive oil, onion and garlic. Chop the spinach and add, along with the chestnuts. Add 2 tablespoons of beaten egg and enough breadcrumbs to form a firm but not too dry paste and season well. Form the mixture into 4 cakes, dust with flour and, one by one, dip into the beaten egg and breadcrumbs. Chill well to firm up.

Meanwhile, make the broth. Heat the butter in a saucepan and cook the parsnip and onion until slightly softened. Add the pickle and enough stock to cover the vegetables by at least 3cm. Stir well, add the potato, season well, add a pinch of sugar and cook until very soft.

When ready to serve, deep- or pan-fry the cakes in a little hot oil until crisp and golden. Spoon a little of the broth into a bowl and top with a cake or cakes and serve immediately.

SERVES: 4
PREPARATION: 10mins
plus 15 minutes soaking
COOKING: 25mins

BAKED RED MULLET WITH MUSHROOMS AND LEMON

I like whole fish on the bone, I think they hold their succulence and flavour when cooked this way. Ask your fishmonger to do all the hard preparation work for you – that way you can just concentrate on the cooking!

4 x 400g red mullet, scaled, gutted and heads off

75g unsalted butter, softened

400ml strong fish stock*

50g dried ceps (porcini)

1 small onion, finely chopped

3 smoked garlic cloves

3 pinches of caster sugar

3 teaspoons white wine vinegar

zest of 2 lemons

2 heaped tablespoons chopped fresh sage

salt and freshly ground black pepper

Preheat the oven to 200°C/400°F/gas mark 6. Place the mullet on two non-stick baking sheets. Smear over 50g of the unsalted butter and season well with salt and pepper.

Bring the fish stock to the boil in a small pan. Place the dried mushrooms in a small bowl and carefully pour the boiling stock over; leave to soak for 15 minutes, or until soft.

Heat 25g of the butter in a saucepan and add the onion and garlic; cook gently for about 5 minutes.

When the mushrooms are soaked, strain them through a fine sieve twice, reserving the liquor. Rinse the mushrooms to remove any grit.

Pour the mushroom and fish stock onto the onions and garlic and bring to the boil. Add the sugar, vinegar and a little salt and pepper. Bring to the boil and then simmer until reduced by half, then add the mushrooms. Cook until you have a thick stew, then remove the pan from the heat. Finally, stir in the lemon zest and chopped sage.

Bake the fish for 18–20 minutes, occasionally spooning the cooking juices over.

Place the mullet onto 4 plates and spoon over the sauce to serve.

* Make the stock up using half the amount of water specified on the pack instructions.

TWICE BAKED PORK WITH RED ONION STIR-FRY

This is a really delicious way to eat belly pork. After the first cooking stage the meat can be chilled well and then warmed through for 30 minutes at 180°C/350°F/gas mark 4, brushed occasionally with the marinade.

For the pork

1kg belly pork, cut into 4 equal pieces, skin removed

1 litre strong pork or chicken stock*

100ml red wine vinegar

2 teaspoons ground cumin

2 pinches of ground allspice

2 pinches of chilli powder

4 tablespoons clear honey

finely grated zest and juice of 1 orange

finely grated zest and juice of 1 lemon

1 teaspoon Sichuan peppercorns, crushed

salt and freshly ground black pepper

For the stir-fry

4 tablespoons olive oil

2 garlic cloves, finely chopped

½ teaspoon ground cumin

½ teaspoon ground allspice

2 large red onions, roughly chopped

2 large sweet potatoes, cut into 2cm cubes

Preheat the oven to 150°C/300°F/gas mark 2. Season the belly pork well with salt and pepper and place in a non-stick roasting tin. Pour the stock over the pork, then cover with foil. Place the tin on the stove and bring to the boil. Once the stock has boiled, cook the pork in the oven for about 2½ hours, or until very soft when pierced with a knife.

Next, make the spicy marinade: place the vinegar, cumin, allspice, chilli, honey, orange zest and juice, lemon zest and juice and crushed peppercorns in a glass bowl and mix well together, then leave to dissolve for 10 minutes.

Increase the oven temperature to 220°C/425°F/gas mark 7. Carefully tip off the hot stock from around the pork and set aside (this freezes well and can be used for soup). Spoon over the spicy marinade and return the tin, uncovered, to the oven. Keep spooning over the marinade during the cooking time until the meat is nicely glazed (about 30 minutes). You will end up with beautifully coloured joints, and just a little marinade left.

Meanwhile, heat the oil in a wok, add the garlic and spices and cook for 2-3 minutes; do not burn. Add the onions and sweet potatoes, season well with salt and pepper, turn down the heat, then cover with a loose-fitting lid or foil. Cook for 15-20 minutes, stirring occasionally. The steam produced from the onions and potatoes will be sufficient to cook them perfectly. Serve the pork with the vegetable stir-fry and any remaining marinade.

* Make the stock up using half the amount of water specified on the pack instructions.

GRILLED RUMP STEAK WITH RED WINE BUTTER

SERVES: 4
PREPARATION: 15mins
COOKING: 5-12mins

I like butters on steak as a change from sauce. The flavoured butter in this recipe turns a plain steak into something quite special - go on, give it a go!

225g unsalted butter, softened

1 tablespoon gluten-free tomato ketchup

2 teaspoons gluten-free English mustard

2 shallots, very finely chopped

2 tablespoons chopped tarragon

1 garlic clove, crushed

½ teaspoon smoked paprika

1 teaspoon gluten-free Worcestershire sauce

2 tablespoons red wine

pinch of curry powder

zest and juice of 1 lemon

salt and freshly ground black pepper

4 x 225g thick-cut British, rump steaks

Much has been written about steaks recently and quite rightly so. Here are my basic rules for buying and preparing: firstly, always buy British - that's an absolute must. Secondly, look for a minimum 21 day-aged steak, 28 days is even better! And always dry the steak well on kitchen towel before cooking – this will ensure a nice colour and prevent it from boiling in a pan or on a grill tray.

Place the softened butter, ketchup, mustard, shallots and paprika in a bowl and beat until creamy and light. Next, add the Worcestershire sauce and red wine and mix well; this will take a couple of minutes. Finally, add the curry powder, lemon zest and juice and a little salt and pepper.

Lay out a 30cm square piece of foil. Spoon the butter onto one end, then carefully roll it up. Twist both ends together, until the roll is tight, then chill really well. The butter will keep in the fridge for up to 1 month, 3 months in the freezer.

Preheat a ridged griddle pan over a high heat and sauté the steaks for 2½ minutes on each side for rare, 4 minutes each side for medium and 6 minutes each side for well done. Allow the steak to rest for 5 minutes. To serve, top each steak with a couple of circles of chilled butter.

ROASTED PUMPKIN AND RED PEPPER DIP

SERVES: 6
PREPARATION: 20mins
COOKING: 50mins

I love this dip, partly because it's so much more than dip – it's also a side dish to serve with sausages or chicken, a cracker topping, a stuffing for chicken or turkey or even a topping for a pizza base.

600g pumpkin, halved, deseeded and cut into wedges

100g pumpkin seeds

2 tablespoons olive oil

4 rashers back bacon, finely chopped

200g Cheddar cheese, finely grated

1 x 350g jar ready-roasted red peppers, finely chopped

1 large garlic clove, finely crushed

4 tablespoons mango chutney

2 tablespoons mayonnaise (check it is a gluten-free variety)

4 tablespoons extra virgin olive oil

salt and freshly ground black pepper

Preheat the oven to 200°C/400°F/gas mark 6. Roast the pumpkin with a generous amount of olive oil and salt and pepper. Roast for 40 minutes. Leave until completely cold.

Using a dessertspoon, carefully spoon out the flesh paring it away from the skin and place it in a large bowl. Gently mash the pumpkin with a potato masher until you have a chunky purée.

Lightly fry the pieces of bacon in a dry non-stick frying pan until the bacon is crispy and well coloured. Add the cooked bacon to the pumpkin.

Add the rest of the ingredients to the bowl, stir well and season with salt and pepper to taste.

It's best to leave the dip for a couple of hours at room temperature to take on a full flavour, before serving.

SERVES: 4
PREPARATION: 20mins
COOKING: 20-25mins

PIL PIL PRAWNS

Yes, 9 cloves of garlic! Yes, the sauce is very oily! But it's beautiful to look at and wonderful to eat - trust me! We used to cook this in my pub a few years ago and it was a great hit - Andy, the chef, really loved it. It's nice eaten hot or cold as a sort of tapas. In fact, I think it's best cooked, cooled and chilled and eaten the next day as all the flavours develop really well – that is if you can wait a day once you get a hint of the fantastic cooking aromas!

The sauce can be used also with pork, chicken or fish.

75ml olive oil

2 red onions, finely chopped

¼ teaspoon dried chilli flakes

9 garlic cloves, finely chopped

1 heaped tablespoon smoked paprika

60g palm sugar

juice of 4 limes

20 freshwater prawns, peeled and de-veined

salt and freshly ground black pepper

steamed rice, to serve

Heat the oil and add the onions, chilli and garlic and cook for 10 minutes to soften well.

Add the paprika and cook for a further 2-3 minutes; do not burn.

Next add the palm sugar and lime juice, season well and turn down the heat. Reduce the total volume of the liquid and onions by roughly half.

Taste the sauce and adjust if you think you have to. It should have a nice balance of sweet and sour.

When you are ready to serve up, bring the sauce to a simmer, then drop in the prawns and cook for 3-4 minutes in total. They will turn from opaque to light pink – be careful not to overcook them or they will be tough.

Serve the prawns in small bowls, with a little steamed rice.

SERVES: 2
PREPARATION: 10mins
COOKING: 15mins

STEAMED MUSSELS WITH SPICY SAUSAGE

This might sound a rather strange combination but it really is very good. The French cook a similar dish with fresh oysters.

2 tablespoons olive oil

1 small onion, finely chopped

2 garlic cloves, crushed

150g spicy sausage, thinly sliced (chorizo is perfect but do check it is a gluten-free variety)

2 glasses medium-dry white wine

½ 10g gluten-free fish stock cube

1½kg fresh mussels, large, closed and well scrubbed

freshly ground black pepper

4 tablespoons chopped fresh flat-leaf parsley

a squeeze of lemon

Heat the olive oil in a large, deep saucepan, add the onion, garlic and spicy sausage and cook, stirring, for 1 minute.

Pour in the white wine and crumble in the fish stock cube, then stir, bring to the boil and cook for 3 minutes.

Add the mussels, cover the pan with a tight-fitting lid and cook for about 4-5 minutes. After this cooking time, when you lift off the lid, your kitchen should be filled with a gorgeous aroma and all the mussels should have opened.

Taste a little of the juice, check the seasoning and adjust if necessary with pepper (you probably won't need any salt).

Using a slotted spoon, divide the cooked mussels between two deep serving bowls, trying to keep as much juice as possible in the pan.

Add the parsley and a squeeze of lemon to the pan and stir well, then ladle the delicious liquor over the mussels and serve immediately.

INDIAN-STYLE POPCORN

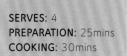

SERVES: 4
PREPARATION: 25mins
COOKING: 30mins

This is a lovely way to enjoy popcorn - my kids love this provided I go easy with the chilli!

2 tablespoons olive oil

4 cardamom pods, crushed

250g popping corn

½ teaspoon salt

½ teaspoon paprika

2 teaspoons dried garlic granules

½ teaspoon cayenne pepper

pinch of chilli powder

Heat the oil in a heavy-based saucepan, taking care not to burn. Add the cardamom pods and the corn, and turn the heat down slightly. Cover tightly with a lid, then leave to cook until all the popping has ceased.

Turn out the hot popcorn, then sprinkle with the salt, paprika, garlic, cayenne and chilli powder. Mix really well and serve hot.

FRESH PEA HOUMOUS

SERVES: 4
PREPARATION: 25mins
COOKING: none

Houmous is a great starter and I love this vibrantly coloured green pea version. The peas simply need defrosting and blitzing with all the other ingredients - simple!

500g frozen peas, defrosted

2 garlic cloves, chopped

2 tablespoons tahini

4 tablespoons chopped fresh parsley

½ teaspoon smoked paprika

3 tablespoons olive oil

2 tablespoons lemon juice

Place the peas, garlic, tahini, parsley and smoked paprika in a food processor, then season and blitz really well until you have a smooth purée.

Gradually add the oil in a thin stream, then add the lemon juice. Spoon into a bowl and check the seasoning and adjust if needed.

Serve with rice crackers, Tarragon Muffins (see page 56) or Drop Scones (see page 159)

DEEP FRIED ARANCINI WITH CHICKPEA DIP

SERVES: 4
PREPARATION: 25mins
COOKING: 45mins

I like these delicious rice balls served with the Chickpea Dip either hot, as part of a buffet, or cold with salad.

1 tablespoon olive oil

½ small onion, very finely chopped

1 small garlic clove, finely chopped

120g arborio rice

1 x 10g gluten-free vegetable stock cube

100ml white wine

30g unsalted butter

100g Parmesan cheese, grated

80g chickpea (gram) flour

2 large eggs, beaten

200g fine polenta or cornmeal

vegetable oil, for deep frying

For the spicy chickpea dip

½ onion, finely chopped

1 garlic clove, finely chopped

pinch of cumin seeds, toasted

pinch of saffron powder

½ teaspoon chopped fresh rosemary

3 tablespoons olive oil

160g tinned chickpeas, drained

2 tablespoons red wine vinegar

3 tablespoons roughly chopped fresh parsley

salt and freshly ground black pepper

Heat the olive oil in a medium saucepan. Cook the onion and the garlic until soft, and then add the rice, stirring to coat well in oil.

Crumble the stock cube over the rice and add the wine. Simmer and reduce until all the liquid is absorbed, stirring all the time. Gradually add the boiling water, a little at a time, stirring well until the rice is just cooked through (15-20 minutes).

Once cooked, and thick, remove from the heat, stir in the butter, cheese and a grind of pepper. Check the seasoning, leave to cool and then chill well.

When chilled, form into balls the size of a small marble. Place the chickpea flour, beaten eggs and polenta or cornmeal in three separate bowls. Roll the rice balls in the chickpea flour, then dip in the egg and finally coat in the polenta or cornmeal

Pour the vegetable oil into a large, deep pan until approximately 2.5cm in depth, then heat to 180°C/350°F. Deep-fry the rice balls for 3-4 minutes or until golden.

To make the Spicy Chickpea Dip, fry the onion, garlic, cumin seeds, saffron and rosemary in half the oil until soft and golden. Add 100g of the chickpeas and cook again for 10 minutes. Blitz in a food processor, taste and adjust the seasoning, and then stir in the parsley and the remaining whole chickpeas. Serve as an accompaniment to the arancini.

SMOKED DUCK ROLLS WITH SWEET RELISH

This is a twist on the classic Chinese duck pancakes. You can buy really nice hot-smoked duck breasts now and they have a deep flavour. The relish is simple - onion marmalade, cooked very slowly until it tastes almost sweet and sour. This is good finger food - great for the kids to get involved.

For the relish

4 tablespoons olive oil

3 medium onions, very finely sliced

2 teaspoons dried thyme

100ml Madeira

1 x 10g gluten-free beef stock cube

2 tablespoons red wine vinegar

salt and freshly ground black pepper

For the rolls

16 rice pancake wrappers

1 large, hot-smoked duck breast, skinned and finely shredded

140g cucumber, cut into 3cm matchsticks

4 tablespoons roughly chopped fresh coriander

For the relish, heat the oil in a small pan then add the onions. Stir well, and then add the thyme. Place a lid on, then turn down the heat and cook very gently for about 45 minutes, stirring occasionally. If you cook the relish too quickly with the lid off, the water in the onions will evaporate too quickly and the onions will be tough, so the longer you cook it for the better.

Once the onions are softened, add the Madeira, crumbled stock cube, vinegar, salt and pepper. Cook down over a slightly higher heat until really thick and moist.

Lay the pancakes out and divide the duck evenly between them. Top with the cucumber and coriander.

Spoon over a little warm relish, wrap up by folding the sides in first, then rolling up. This will make sure the filling does not spill out.

GLUTEN-FREE PIZZA BASE

MAKES: 2 x 20cm bases
PREPARATION: 15mins plus 15mins rising
COOKING: 30mins

Of all the recipes, this one was the hardest to get right. It takes a lot to get a new recipe past my kids, but in the end they loved it.

1 teaspoon sugar

300ml lukewarm water

2 x 7g sachets dried yeast

300g gluten-free flour (see Gluten-Free Flour Mix, page 152)

1 teaspoon xanthan gum

1 level teaspoon gluten-free baking powder

1 teaspoon salt

1 tablespoon olive oil

topping ingredients of your choice

Dissolve the sugar in half the warm water, stir in the yeast, mix well and set aside for 5 minutes for the yeast to start work and froth.

Place the remaining dry ingredients in a large mixing bowl, add the yeast mixture and oil and mix well, adding the remaining water a little at a time. Mix through until you have a smooth, fairly wet dough.

Cover the bowl with a clean cloth and allow the dough to rise in a warm place for about 15 minutes.

Preheat the oven to 200°C/400°F/gas mark 6.

Divide the dough into two balls. Transfer one dough ball onto a sheet of baking parchment. Cover with a second sheet of parchment on top and flatten the dough out between the papers, to form a 20cm circle. Repeat to make another base.

Transfer the bases onto baking trays. Bake the pizza for 8-10 minutes and then remove to add the toppings of your choice.

Return the pizzas to the oven, with the toppings and bake for a further 15-20 minutes until bubbling and golden. Serve hot, straight away.

POLENTA-CRUSTED PARSLEY ONION RINGS

These are nice served with steak and chips or as a starter. Just remember not to cook too many at once or they won't cook properly.

vegetable oil for deep frying
85g chickpea (gram) flour
100g fine polenta or cornmeal
4 tablespoons roughly chopped fresh parsley
1 large onion, sliced into ½cm rings
150ml milk
salt and freshly ground black pepper

Place the chickpea flour in a bowl. Place the polenta in a separate bowl, add the chopped parsley and season well. Pour the milk into another bowl, and then add a little salt and pepper.

Place the onion rings in the chickpea flour, then into the milk and then into the polenta and parsley mixture, taking care to coat evenly.

Pour the vegetable oil into a deep fryer or a large, deep pan until approximately 2.5cm in depth, then heat to 190°C/375°F or until a cube of bread browns in 30-40 seconds.

Cook the rings in batches: carefully place 6–8 onion rings into the hot oil using a metal spoon. Cook for 3-5 minutes, turning once, until crisp and golden. Drain well on kitchen paper. Keep the cooked rings hot on a warm plate, covered with foil and cook the remaining rings.

WASABI CUCUMBER SHRIMP CRACKERS

MAKES: 20
PREPARATION: 15mins
COOKING: none

I like wasabi but it needs really careful handling - too much and it's awful, too little and you cannot taste it. Japanese flavours should be really clear and tasty and these crackers are a simple twist on prawn cocktail.

225g cooked prawns, chopped

4 tablespoons mayonnaise (check it is a gluten-free variety)

2 spring onions, very finely chopped

2 teaspoons wasabi

2 teaspoons chopped pickled ginger

2 tablespoons finely chopped skin-on cucumber

20 square thin rice cakes

pinch of cayenne pepper

salt and freshly ground black pepper

Stir the chopped prawns into the mayonnaise, add the spring onions, and a good seasoning of salt and pepper.

Add the wasabi, ginger and cucumber and mix well.

Spoon onto the cut rice crackers, and sprinkle with a little cayenne pepper, or serve as a dip with crackers around it. Serve straight away.

VEGETARIAN

THE RECIPES: ROASTED CHICKPEAS WITH TOMATOES AND TALEGGIO / TURKISH ROASTED VEGETABLES WITH THICK YOGURT / GLAZED RED ONIONS WITH TOFU AND SALSA VERDE / SLOW-COOKED AUBERGINES WITH YOGURT / SWEET AND SOUR CELERY HEARTS WITH AUBERGINES / DEEP-FRIED COURGETTE WEDGES WITH SPICY COLESLAW / BLACK OLIVE MASH WITH SOFT-BOILED EGGS AND PEPPERS / AUBERGINE CANNELLONI WITH BEETROOT SALSA / CURRY PILAF WITH CASHEWS

ROASTED CHICKPEAS WITH TOMATOES AND TALEGGIO

This is a dip-come-salad-come-vegetable accompaniment - quite unusual, and very nice to graze on. Any cheese will do, but I love the creamy taleggio with the tomatoes and peppers. I like to serve this as a starter or as an accompaniment to grilled or barbecued meats or fish.

2 x 240g tins chickpeas, rinsed and drained

8 tablespoons olive oil

1 x 410g tin cannellini beans, rinsed and well drained

2 tablespoons tomato purée

2 tablespoons balsamic vinegar

1 garlic clove, finely chopped

150g taleggio cheese, cut into small pieces

150g roasted red peppers from a jar, cut into thick strips

200g semi-dried tomatoes, cut into 2 or 3 pieces

salt and freshly ground black pepper

Preheat the oven to 220ºC/425ºF/gas mark 7.

Toss the chickpeas and 3 tablespoons of olive oil together well, then add a little salt and pepper and mix well.

Spoon into a baking tray, then roast in the hot oven for 15-20 minutes to brown nicely. Stir occasionally.

Meanwhile, purée the beans with the remaining olive oil, tomato purée, vinegar, garlic and salt and pepper. You may need to add a little more oil to get a dropping consistency.

Once the chickpeas are cooked, spoon into a bowl and pour over the purée mixture, mix well and cool to room temperature.

Once cooled, add the cheese, peppers and tomatoes. Mix well, but carefully.

TURKISH ROASTED VEGETABLES WITH THICK YOGURT

SERVES: 4
PREPARATION: 45mins
COOKING: 1 hour

The key to this dish is to roast the vegetables in small batches as if you roast them all in one tin, the temperature will drop and they will sweat and not roast properly. I think this dish is best left overnight to allow the flavours to develop and then re-warmed - great as a starter or a main course.

For the vegetables
100g courgettes, cut into large strips
125g aubergines, cut into long strips
100g green peppers, cut into 2cm strips
6 tablespoons olive oil
1 medium onion, sliced into thin wedges
1 teaspoon chopped garlic
150g swede, cut into 2cm x 5cm strips
200g potatoes, cut into 2cm cubes
150g carrots, cut into 4cm x 1cm strips
½ teaspoon coriander seeds, crushed
pinch of ground allspice

salt and ground white pepper

For the tomato sauce
300ml tomato juice
40g sugar
40ml red wine vinegar
80g tinned chickpeas, drained

To serve
200g natural yogurt
3 tablespoons roughly chopped fresh coriander
olive oil, to drizzle

Preheat the oven to 220°C/425°F/gas mark 7. Place the courgettes, aubergines and peppers in a deep roasting tin and drizzle with 2 tablespoons of the oil.

Place the onion and the garlic in a separate roasting tin and drizzle with 2 tablespoons of the oil.

Place the swede, potatoes and carrots in another roasting tin and drizzle with the last of the oil. Sprinkle a few coriander seeds and some allspice over all the vegetables, season well and stir thoroughly. Roast all the vegetables until they are cooked, about 30 minutes.

Next, place the tomato juice, sugar and vinegar in a pan, season and then cook down to roughly half the original volume. At that point, re-season and add the chickpeas, mixing in well. All the above steps can be done well in advance.

Finally, combine all the vegetables, stir through the tomato sauce and re-season. To serve, place the roasted mixture just warmed through, in a large bowl, top with natural yogurt, fresh coriander and a drizzle of olive oil.

GLAZED RED ONIONS WITH TOFU AND SALSA VERDE

I think tofu gets a lot of bad press; it's a great basic ingredient to add a variety of flavours to. Smoked tofu is rather tasty, and let's not forget, also very good for you. Roasted onions I adore, and this way they really are full of flavour. Served with the tofu, they make a rather special vegetarian meal.

6 unpeeled large red onions

2 teaspoons caster sugar

85g unsalted butter

4 tablespoons olive oil

200g smoked tofu, cut into 1cm cubes, then patted dry

salt and freshly ground black pepper

For the salsa verde

5 tablespoons chopped fresh parsley

8 tablespoons chopped fresh basil

2 garlic cloves, chopped

2 tablespoons drained capers

100ml extra virgin olive oil

pinch of hot chilli powder

Preheat the oven to 200°C/400°F/gas mark 6. Place a wire cooling rack in a roasting tin. Place the onions on the cooling rack. Roast in the oven for 1½ hours. To check if the onions are cooked, a knife should be able to pass through the flesh and skin with very little resistance. Set aside to cool. Once cooled, carefully remove the outer leaves until you get to the soft flesh.

Next, make the salsa verde, by placing all the ingredients into a food processor and blitz until you have a chunky purée. Check the seasoning and adjust if needed.

Back to the onions, cut them in half lengthways, and then sprinkle the cut side with a little salt, pepper and sugar. Heat the unsalted butter in a non-stick frying pan until it starts to brown slightly, then gently cook the onions, cut-side down in the butter, until they are nicely browned. Take care, as the onions will brown quickly due to the added sugar, plus their own natural sugar.

Meanwhile, heat the olive oil in a wok or frying pan and add the dry tofu. Season well with salt and pepper, and cook over a high heat to colour.

To serve, place 3 halves of warm onion on each of 4 plates, then spoon over the cooked tofu and the salsa verde.

SLOW-COOKED AUBERGINES WITH YOGURT

SERVES: 4
PREPARATION: 15mins
COOKING: 45mins -
1 hour

Aubergines have little flavour on their own, but you can make them really tasty. I believe that the best way to cook them is really slowly, covered, in the oven. Also, I think you need to add big flavours to the mix. This recipe is a great main course, but also a nice salad with a boiled egg or two.

100ml olive oil

2 onions, roughly chopped

2 aubergines, cut into 2cm cubes

4 garlic cloves, finely chopped

2 teaspoons smoked paprika

1 teaspoon dried oregano

pinch or two of chilli powder

4 tablespoons chopped fresh mint

6 tablespoons chopped fresh basil

12 cherry plum tomatoes, halved

4 tablespoons chopped fresh coriander

salt and freshly ground black pepper

gluten-free crackers and natural Greek yogurt,
    to serve

Preheat the oven to 200°C/400°F/gas mark 6.

Heat the olive oil in a medium flameproof casserole dish, then add the onions and cook over a fairly high heat until coloured nicely.

Add the aubergines, garlic, paprika, oregano, chilli, fresh mint and seasoning. Mix really well, then cover and cook in the oven for 45 minutes to an hour, or until very soft and almost pulpy.

Once cooked, remove from the oven, uncover and stir well. Check the seasoning. Stir through the fresh basil, tomatoes and coriander but do not overmix.

Serve with gluten-free crackers, topped with a spoonful of yogurt.

SWEET AND SOUR CELERY HEARTS WITH AUBERGINES

When I was a young cook, celery hearts were all the rage, and we cooked them many times in the hotel where I worked. They seem to have fallen out of favour now – it's a shame as they are so delicious.

6 tablespoons olive oil

½ teaspoon chilli powder

½ teaspoon paprika

½ teaspoon ground turmeric

½ teaspoon ground cumin

2 garlic cloves, chopped

1 large onion, finely chopped

1 small aubergine, cut into 2cm cubes

1 tablespoon tomato purée

4 small celery hearts

1 x 10g gluten-free vegetable stock cube

2 tablespoons clear honey

2 tablespoons lime juice

2 tablespoons tamarind paste

salt and freshly ground black pepper

Preheat the oven to 200°C/400°F/gas mark 6. Heat the oil in a flameproof casserole dish, then add the spices and cook them gently to release their flavours.

Add the garlic and onion and coat well in the spicy oil.

Add the aubergine and tomato purée, then mix well. Place the celery hearts on top of the onions and aubergines.

Crumble over the stock cube, honey, lime juice and tamarind paste, then season well with salt and pepper.

Cover with a tight-fitting lid and pop into the oven. Cook for 50 minutes to an hour, or until the celery hearts are fully cooked.

Once cooked, if the mixture seems too moist, then gently cook over a low heat on the stove to thicken slightly, stirring occasionally.

Spoon the aubergines into deep serving bowls and top with a braised celery heart.

DEEP-FRIED COURGETTE WEDGES WITH SPICY COLESLAW

When I was an apprentice, fried courgettes were really new and modern; they can be really nice, but also really awful - you need to make sure the oil is hot and you fry them in batches for a great result. Coleslaw, I love and this is the original way to make it - with oil and vinegar. These ingredients were used for a specific reason.

For the coleslaw

½ small Savoy cabbage, very finely sliced

1 tablespoon chopped fresh ginger

2 teaspoons sesame oil

4 tablespoons olive oil

5 tablespoons rice vinegar

2 teaspoons caster sugar

salt and freshly ground black pepper

pinch or two of chilli powder

For the courgettes

2 large courgettes, thoroughly washed

2 tablespoons chickpea (gram) flour

4 eggs, lightly beaten

300g fine cornmeal

2 tablespoons black onion seeds

rapeseed oil, for deep frying

The first thing to do is to make the salad: place the cabbage and ginger in a large bowl and whisk the oils, vinegar, sugar, salt, pepper and chilli powder in a jug. Pour over the cabbage and ginger and mix well. Leave to wilt for 30-40 minutes.

Cut the courgettes into thickish wedges. Place the flour and beaten egg in separate bowls. Combine the cornmeal and onion seeds in a third bowl.

Place the courgette wedges in the chickpea flour and coat well. Then place in the beaten egg, then into the cornmeal and onion seeds, coating well.

Pour the rapeseed oil into a deep-fryer or a large, deep pan until approximately 2.5cm in depth, then heat to 180°C/350°F or until a cube of bread browns in 10 seconds.

Deep-fry the courgette wedges in small batches, until golden, then dust with salt, place on a warm plate and cover with foil to keep hot whilst you cook the remaining wedges. Serve with the spicy coleslaw.

OLIVE MASH WITH SOFT-BOILED EGGS AND PEPPERS

SERVES: 4
PREPARATION: 20mins
COOKING: 25mins

When we were children my mum would cook mashed potatoes and my father would then peel a soft-boiled egg and pop it on top. This dish is a great, easy starter or main course; the mash, coupled with spicy pepperdew peppers and black olives, then topped with a soft-boiled egg is, to me, delicious.

500g potatoes, roughly chopped

75g butter, melted

200ml warm milk

50g pitted black olives, roughly chopped

150g spicy pepperdew peppers, quartered

4 tablespoons chopped fresh parsley

4 soft-boiled eggs (cooked for 4 minutes), shelled carefully and left whole

salt and freshly ground black pepper

celery salt, to serve

Place the potatoes in cold water, add a little salt, bring to the boil, then simmer for 20 minutes or until very soft.

Drain well and return the potatoes to the pan. Place the pan over a very low heat and drive off all the leftover water; this will only take a few seconds.

Mash with a potato masher, and then add all the melted butter and enough warm milk to give a smooth, creamy consistency. Add a little salt and pepper to taste, then whisk the mash. I like to hand whisk my mash to make it light and fluffy but a wooden spoon will work just as well.

Fold in the olives, peppers and parsley, mix really well and adjust the seasoning if needed. Divide the mash between 4 plates and top with a boiled egg. Serve with a dusting of celery salt.

AUBERGINE CANNELLONI WITH BEETROOT SALSA

I once cooked this for some Italian friends and they loved it. The great combination of Italian cheeses and vegetables mixed together carefully makes a fab veggie main course.

For the cannelloni

8 tablespoons olive oil, plus extra for greasing
   and brushing
1 large aubergine, sliced lengthways into 8
150g ricotta cheese
100g Parmesan cheese
pinch of dried oregano
2 garlic cloves, chopped
4 tablespoons chopped fresh chives
100g cooked basmati rice

1 medium egg, well beaten
16 fresh basil leaves
salt and ground white pepper

For the beetroot salsa

4 large cooked beetroots, cut into ½cm cubes
250g cherry tomatoes, halved
4 tablespoons olive oil
2 tablespoons chopped fresh basil
2 tablespoons sherry vinegar
freshly ground black pepper

Preheat the oven to 200°C/400°F/gas mark 6. Lightly oil a 24 x 24 x 4cm baking dish. Heat 2 tablespoons of olive oil for the cannelloni in a frying pan. Then add a couple of slices of aubergine, and cook for 2-3 minutes on each side, until lightly coloured and soft in texture. Drain well on kitchen paper, and then season well. Repeat with the remaining aubergine.

Place the cheeses, oregano, garlic, chives, cooked rice and egg in a bowl, season with salt and white pepper and mix really well. Lay out the slices of cooked aubergine on a chopping board.

Spoon the rice mixture onto the 8 slices at one end, lay 2 basil leaves on each aubergine slice, and then carefully roll up, Swiss-roll style. Pack into a lightly oiled baking tray, oil well and season with salt and pepper. Pop into the oven, and cook for 20 minutes.

Meanwhile, place the cooked beetroot, cherry tomatoes, oil, basil and sherry vinegar in a bowl, season with salt and black pepper and mix really well. Leave the salsa to marinate whilst the cannelloni cook.

Once the aubergine rolls are cooked, remove from the oven, spoon over the beetroot salsa and let your guests help themselves from the baking dish.

CURRY PILAF WITH CASHEWS

SERVES: 4 as a main course or 8 as a starter
PREPARATION: 14mins
COOKING: 4mins

I like rice dishes in any shape or form. This is a twist on a curry without the meat or fish, combining rice and spices, pushing the pilaf a little further. Purists may sneer, but it's a delicious veggie starter or main course.

2 tablespoons olive oil

2 small courgettes, chopped

½ x 410g tin chickpeas, rinsed and drained

100g frozen peas

1 medium red onion, chopped

½ teaspoon dried chilli flakes

2 teaspoons cumin seeds

1 teaspoon turmeric

225g basmati rice

100ml white wine

1 x 10g vegetable gluten-free stock cube

4 tablespoons chopped coriander

25g unsalted butter

110g cashew nuts

salt and freshly ground black pepper

gluten-free rice crackers or poppadums, to serve

Preheat the oven to 200°C/400°F/gas mark 6. Heat the olive oil in a large flameproof casserole dish, add the courgettes, chickpeas and peas and cook for a couple of minutes to give them a little colour.

Add the onion and spices and cook gently for about 5 minutes until soft. Add the rice and stir well to coat in the oil, then add the wine, crumbled stock cube and 600ml water. Season well then bring to the boil, stirring all the time.

Cover the dish with a tight-fitting lid and cook in the oven for 14–16 minutes, or until the rice is tender. Once cooked, remove from the oven and stir well.

Add the coriander, butter and nuts, then stir well and re-cover and leave for 5 minutes. Serve the pilaf with rice crackers or poppadums.

CAKES, PASTRIES, BISCUITS & DESSERTS

THE RECIPES: GLUTEN-FREE FLOUR MIX / GLUTEN-FREE PASTRY / MOIST FRUIT CAKE / SOFT GINGERBREAD / SOFT LEMON AND LIME BAR CAKES / BLUEBERRY CHEESECAKE BAR CAKE / MILLIONAIRE'S SHORTBREAD WITH BRAMLEY APPLE DIP / ORANGE AND LIME SHORTBREAD / DROP SCONES / SESAME AND BLACK PEPPER LACE BISCUITS / POLENTA TRAY BAKE WITH TANGY FRUIT FONDANT / RICH CHOCOLATE BROWNIES WITH CARAMEL SAUCE / BITTER CHOCOLATE AND CHERRY MUFFINS / PLAIN SCONES / FUDGY ALMOND CAKE WITH MINT SYRUP AND FROSTING / SQUIDGY CHESTNUT MERINGUE CAKE / BIRTHDAY CAKE SPONGE / EASY ICED BLACKCURRANT MOUSSE / RED WINE SYLLABUB WITH RAISINS / BAKEWELL PUDDING (TART) / WARM MOUSSELINE GLAZED MANDARINS / TOFFEE RIPPLE CHEESECAKE WITH BLUEBERRY STEW / TANGY LIME MOUSSE WITH MINT MUDDLE / REALLY EASY CHOCOLATE MOUSSE / BRAMLEY APPLE AND PEAR CRUMBLE / ROASTED PEACHES WITH BUTTERSCOTCH / CAROLE'S NO-FLOUR ORANGE CAKE / BAKED INDIAN RICE PUDDING WITH NUTS, FRUIT AND SAFFRON / LIGHT PINK GRAPEFRUIT MOUSSE / OVEN-POACHED RHUBARB WITH MOUSSELINE SAUCE

GLUTEN-FREE FLOUR MIX

I've tried many versions of this recipe, chopping and changing all sorts until I got the perfect formula! It is a good alternative to normal gluten-based flours and if you want an alternative to regular self-raising flour, simply add 50g gluten-free baking powder.

300g fine cornmeal (maize) or chestnut flour
500g brown rice flour
200g cornflour

Mix all the flours together very thoroughly or put into a food processor and pulse until mixed. Store in an airtight container for up to 6 months.

GLUTEN-FREE PASTRY

Without gluten, pastry tends to crumble easily, so it's better adapted to recipes where you can press it into the base rather than rolling it out.

225g gluten-free flour mix (see above)
100g butter or margarine, chilled and cut into
   small cubes
1 teaspoon xanthan gum

pinch of salt
1 medium egg
oil or butter, for greasing

Preheat the oven to 190°C/375°F/gas mark 5. Grease a 23cm round tin. Put all the ingredients, except the egg, into a food processor and mix until you have fine crumbs. Add the egg and pulse until the mixture comes together. You may have to add a few drops of cold water. Tip out onto a work surface and knead into a smoothish, soft dough.

Shape the dough into a squat sausage, cut out circles and use to press into the base and sides of the tin (use a little rice flour on your hands to stop it from sticking). Line the pastry case with baking parchment and baking beans. Bake for 15 minutes.

MOIST FRUIT CAKE

MAKES: 1 x 23cm round pastry case
PREPARATION: 20mins, plus 1 hour soaking
COOKING: 1 hour

The secret to a nice, moist fruit cake is to soak the dried fruit before cooking. Here the fruit is boiled, then left to cool and plumped up until it is nice and juicy. If you use dried fruit in a cake the end result can be dry, due to the fruit rehydrating itself once cooked and soaking up all the moisture from the end product. Soaking is always best, especially with Christmas cakes! This cake is also very nice served with vanilla ice cream as a dessert.

450g mixed dried fruit

50g natural glacé cherries, chopped

225g unsalted butter, cut into small cubes

250g caster sugar

2 large eggs, beaten

2 tablespoons black treacle

290g gluten-free flour mix (see recipe on page 152)

1½ teaspoons bicarbonate of soda

1½ teaspoons cream of tartar

1 teaspoon xanthan gum

2 teaspoons mixed spice (check it is a gluten-free variety)

melted butter and gluten-free flour, to prepare the tin

Place the fruit, butter, sugar and 200ml cold water in a stainless steel pan and bring to the boil, stirring. Boil for 5 minutes, stirring occasionally. Cover and set aside until cold.

Preheat the oven to 180°C/350°F/gas mark 4. Line a 23cm round, 8cm deep, springform cake tin with a layer of baking parchment, brush with melted butter and then dust with a little gluten-free flour.

Place the cold fruit mixture in a large bowl. Add the remaining ingredients and mix well. Spoon the mixture into the prepared tin.

Cook until well risen and dark brown, about 1 hour, but don't be tempted to open the oven door too much or the cake will sink in the centre.

Remove from the oven and cool completely. Wrapped in foil the cake will keep for up to 1 week.

MAKES: 18
PREPARATION: 15-20 mins
COOKING: 30mins

SOFT GINGERBREAD

Having worked in Grasmere, Cumbria, the home of the famous gingerbread, I really had to include a recipe for it. This version is made with gluten-free shortbread crumb and is delicious.

For the shortbread crumbs

100g cornflour

100g rice flour

80g unrefined caster sugar

100g butter, chilled and cut into small cubes

For the gingerbread

150g demerara sugar

3 teaspoons ground ginger

55g crystallised ginger, chopped

70g gluten-free flour mix (see recipe on page 152)

½ teaspoon gluten-free baking powder

55g golden syrup

55g black treacle

85g butter

Preheat the oven to 200ºC/400ºF/gas mark 6. Place the cornflour, rice flour and caster sugar in a food processor and blend well. Add the cubed butter and blitz until the mixture resembles fine breadcrumbs.

Pour in 3-4 tablespoons water and pulse until the mixture starts to form a dough. Turn out and press into a 20 x 30cm baking tin. Bake the shortbread layer for about 15 minutes until golden and leave to cool in the tin. Remove from the tin.

Turn the oven down to 180ºC/350ºF/gas mark 4. Line the 20 x 30cm baking tin with baking parchment for the gingerbread.

Place 300g of the cooled shortbread in a food processor with the demerara sugar and process into fine crumbs. Add the ground ginger, crystallised ginger, gluten-free flour and baking powder and pulse to mix well.

In a large pan warm the syrup, treacle and butter together until the butter is melted. Add the crumb mixture and mix thoroughly, using a large spoon.

Press the mixture into the lined tin and press down flat with the back of a spoon. Bake for 15 minutes and then cool in the tin before cutting into small squares.

CUSTARD COOKIES

SERVES: makes 15
PREPARATION: 15 minutes plus 1 hour chilling time
COOKING: 10-15mins

I once worked with a French pastry chef who would make these for the kitchen and I've never forgotten their taste and texture. Of course they were not gluten-free and it's taken me quite some time to adapt the recipe, but now I think I've got it right.

15g (Bird's) custard powder

1 teaspoon sugar

100ml milk

110g unsalted butter, softened

110g caster sugar

90g gluten-free white chocolate, finely chopped

200g sorghum-blend flour (see below)

1 level teaspoon gluten-free baking powder

Place the custard powder and sugar in a bowl and stir in 1 tablespoon milk. Place the remaining milk in a saucepan and heat until just before it starts boiling, then pour onto the custard paste and stir well. Return the custard to the saucepan, place over a gentle heat and bring back to the boil, stirring until thick. Transfer to a bowl and set aside to cool.

Place the butter and sugar in a large bowl and cream together with a wooden spoon until white and fluffy. Beat in the cooled custard paste and then the chocolate, flour and baking powder, stirring well until you have a soft dough. Turn the dough out onto a sheet of clingfilm and roll into a sausage shape, roughly 5cm in diameter. Wrap in the clingfilm and chill or freeze for one hour, until hard enough to slice.

Preheat the oven to 180°C/375°C/gas mark 4. When the dough is very cold, cut into 1cm thick slices, peel off the wrapping and place onto a baking sheet lined with parchment paper. Bake in the oven for about 15 minutes, until the edges are just golden, then remove from the oven and cool slightly before lifting off the tray.

SORGHUM-BLEND FLOUR MIX

MAKES: 500g
PREPARATION: 5mins
COOKING: none

175g sorghum flour

175g potato starch

150g tapioca flour

Sieve all the flours together very thoroughly and evenly, or put into a food processor and pulse until mixed. Store in an airtight container for up to 6 months.

MAKES: 10 bars
PREPARATION: 10mins
COOKING: 30-35mins

BLUEBERRY CHEESECAKE BAR CAKE

Bar cakes are all the rage in America. I really like this soft blueberry cheesecake version with a cup of tea!

1 quantity Orange and Lime Shortbread dough
   (see page 159)
400g cream cheese
2 medium eggs
2 teaspoons vanilla extract
170g caster sugar
75g semi-dried blueberries
icing sugar, to dust

Preheat the oven to 190ºC/375ºF/gas mark 5. Roll out the shortbread dough into a squat sausage shape, cut out circles and use to press into the base of a loose-bottomed 21 x 29 x 3cm tin. Trim off any excess dough, don't worry too much about the look.

Press the dough down and prick it all over with a fork. Bake for about 12 minutes until just cooked and slightly brown. Leave to cool.

In a bowl, whisk the cream cheese until really creamy and light, about 5 minutes. Add the eggs, vanilla and sugar and beat well.

Fold in the blueberries and then pour over the shortbread base.

Cook for 15-20 minutes; do not overcook – it should still be slightly wobbly when you remove it from the oven. Cool completely before taking out of the tin, dust well with icing sugar and slice into 10 bars.

MAKES: 8-12 pieces
PREPARATION: 10mins plus 1-2 hours chilling and setting
COOKING: 35mins

MILLIONAIRE'S SHORTBREAD WITH BRAMLEY APPLE DIP

What a lovely combination: sweet, creamy, chocolate matched with the tartness of the Bramley apple dip. It's just superb!

For the base

150g brown rice flour

55g caster sugar

115g unsalted butter

oil or butter, for greasing

For the filling

150g unsalted butter

150g soft dark brown sugar

397g tin condensed milk

For the topping

200g milk chocolate, broken into pieces

55g white chocolate, broken into pieces (optional)

For the dip

4 large Bramley apples, peeled and cored

150g caster sugar

1 teaspoon ground cinnamon

finely grated zest and juice of 1 lemon

finely grated zest and juice of 1 orange

Preheat the oven to 180°C/350°F/gas mark 4. Grease and line a 20cm square tin with baking parchment. To make the base, mix the rice flour and sugar together and then rub in the butter until it resembles coarse breadcrumbs. Press this mixture very lightly and evenly into the tin and bake for about 15-20 minutes or until pale golden.

To make the filling, place the butter and sugar in a large non-stick frying pan and stir over a medium heat until the butter melts and the sugar dissolves. To make a golden caramel, add the condensed milk, stirring continuously, until the first bubbles appear on the surface. Remove from the heat as soon as it comes to the boil. Spread the caramel evenly over the shortbread base and then cool and chill for about 30 minutes.

Place the apples, sugar, cinnamon, lemon and orange zest and juice in a medium pan and cook down until the apples are cooked. The mixture should be slightly dry, not too wet. Cool and set aside. Place the milk and white chocolate (if using) in 2 separate heatproof bowls. Place the bowls over two pans of barely simmering water to melt the chocolate.

Pour the melted milk chocolate over the cooled caramel, smoothing to the edges. Quickly pour over the white chocolate and gently swirl to create a marbled effect. Allow to set. When the chocolate has set, cut the shortbread into squares and serve with the dip.

ORANGE AND LIME SHORTBREAD

MAKES: 12 small biscuits
PREPARATION: 5mins
COOKING: 10mins

This has a wonderful tangy flavour to contrast with the richness of the shortbread.

100g cornflour

100g rice flour

80g unrefined caster sugar

100g butter, chilled and cut into small cubes

juice of 1 small lime

finely grated zest of 1 small orange

cornflour, for rolling out

oil or butter, for greasing

icing sugar, for dusting

Preheat the oven to 200°C/400°F/gas mark 6. Grease a baking tray. Place the cornflour, rice flour and sugar in a food processor and blend well. Add the cubed butter and blitz until you have fine breadcrumbs.

Add the lime juice and orange zest and mix again. Turn out and knead together well. Roll out quickly and evenly, using a little cornflour if necessary. Using a 6cm round biscuit cutter, cut out 12 biscuits and place on the baking tray. Bake for 10-12 minutes, then cool on the baking tray before carefully lifting off. Dust well with icing sugar to serve.

DROP SCONES

MAKES: 12 small biscuits
PREPARATION: 5mins
COOKING: 10mins

140g gluten-free flour mix (see recipe on page 152)

2 pinches of cream of tartar

2 pinches of bicarbonate of soda

salt and freshly ground black pepper

1 medium egg, lightly beaten

1 tablespoon gluten-free wholegrain mustard

8 tablespoons milk (approximately)

2 tablespoons chopped fresh coriander

vegetable oil, for frying

Place the flour mix, cream of tartar, bicarbonate of soda and seasoning in a bowl and mix well. Add the egg and mustard and mix well, and then add enough milk to form a thickish batter, so it holds its own weight, like thick double cream. Finally, add the chopped coriander.

Heat a little vegetable oil in a large non-stick frying pan. Place 2 tablespoons of the batter in the hot oil. Cook for 2-3 minutes until the sides and top are just set, then flip over and cook for a further 1-2 minutes to set. Repeat until all the batter is used up.

MAKES: 16 biscuits
PREPARATION: 10mins
COOKING: 8–10mins

SESAME AND BLACK PEPPER LACE BISCUITS

These biscuits are very similar to brandy snaps - with a delicious snap and taste when you bite into them. The cracked black pepper adds an extra bite to the biscuits.

125g icing sugar

25g unsalted butter

3 tablespoons clear honey

30g rice flour

1 teaspoon cracked black pepper

1 teaspoon xanthan gum

200g sesame seeds

salt

Preheat the oven to 190ºC/375ºF/gas mark 5. Line a baking tray with baking parchment.

Place the icing sugar, butter, honey and 2 tablespoons water in a medium non-stick pan. Heat gently then bring to the boil, stirring well for 1 minute.

Remove the pan from the heat, stir in the rice flour, black pepper, xanthan gum, sesame seeds and salt. Mix well and then cool to room temperature.

Use a couple of teaspoons to form the mixture into 4cm diameter balls and place on the lined baking tray. Flatten slightly with the back of a spoon and leave enough space around them to allow for spreading.

Cook the biscuits for 8–10 minutes or until well spread out and an even colour. Leave to cool on the baking tray.

POLENTA TRAY BAKE WITH TANGY FRUIT FONDANT

Tray bakes are quick to make, easy to serve and always look great when decorated. The raspberry fondant tops the sponge nicely in this recipe and if you leave it for 30 minutes or so the raspberry and fondant soak into the sponge, making it a real get-your-fingers-sticky cake!

For the sponge

175g unsalted butter, at room temperature

225g caster sugar

3 medium eggs, beaten

3 teaspoons gluten-free baking powder

zest of 1 large lemon

2 teaspoons vanilla extract

250g fine polenta

500g fresh raspberries

butter, for greasing

For the fondant

4 tablespoons fresh lime juice

250g fondant icing sugar

Preheat the oven to 180ºC/350ºF/gas mark 4 and lightly grease a 20 x 24cm baking tin.

Place the butter and sugar in a mixing bowl and lightly cream them together. Add the eggs, baking powder, lemon zest, vanilla and polenta and mix well. Add half the raspberries and carefully fold in.

Spoon into the prepared tin and bake until well risen, about 20 minutes. Leave to cool.

In a medium bowl, mix the lime juice and fondant icing sugar until it is the consistency of very thick cream. Spoon half the icing over the sponge, then top with the remaining raspberries. Drizzle over the rest of the fondant icing and leave to set at room temperature.

RICH CHOCOLATE BROWNIES WITH CARAMEL SAUCE

SERVES: 4-6
PREPARATION: 20mins plus chilling
COOKING: 25-35mins

Brownies are always popular and delicious they are too; I think the squidgier the better! The golden rule is to leave them to cool completely before you try and cut and eat them. I know it's going over the top, but I like to serve mine with ice cream and Carnation Caramel. This is basically cooked condensed milk in a can - it's delicious and widely available from supermarkets.

40g golden syrup

110g unsalted butter

175g caster sugar

160g gluten-free dark chocolate (minimum 70 per cent cocoa solids), broken into pieces

4 eggs

20g rice flour

20g chickpea (gram) flour

1 teaspoon xanthan gum

25g sultanas

1 teaspoon cinnamon

1 teaspoon ground cardamom

25g white chocolate, broken into pieces

50ml brandy

finely grated zest of 1 large orange

397g tin Carnation Caramel (dulce de leche)

icing sugar and vanilla ice cream, to serve

Preheat the oven to 180°C/350°F/gas mark 4. Line a 15 x 20 x 4cm baking tin with baking parchment. Place the golden syrup, butter, sugar and dark chocolate in a heatproof bowl and place over a pan of simmering water to melt.

Place the eggs in a bowl and break up with a whisk. Then add the melted mixture and mix well. Add the flours, xanthan gum, sultanas, spices, white chocolate, brandy and orange zest and mix well, but do not overwork.

Pour into the prepared tin, then pop into the oven and cook for 25-35 minutes. Meanwhile, spoon the Carnation Caramel into a bowl and whisk well.

Once cooked, remove from the oven and cool well before cutting.

Serve at room temperature, dusted with icing sugar, with the sauce and ice cream.

BITTER CHOCOLATE AND CHERRY MUFFINS

Muffins are generally easy to make – they are very popular and great if you want to get the kids involved. The irony here is that the enemy of the humble muffin is gluten! The more you mix flour in a regular recipe, the tighter the mixture becomes and you end up with a tough chewy sponge. So I think gluten-free muffins actually have a better texture!

150g fine cornmeal (maize flour)

100g gluten-free flour mix (see recipe on page 152)

2 teaspoons gluten-free baking powder

150g caster sugar

1½ teaspoons xanthan gum

4 tablespoons olive oil

1 medium egg

250ml milk

100g glacé cherries, chopped

75g gluten-free dark chocolate (minimum 70 per cent cocoa solids), broken into pieces

salt

Preheat the oven to 200°C/400°F/gas mark 6. Place 8 paper muffin cases in a muffin tray.

Place the cornmeal, flour mix, baking powder, sugar, xanthan gum and a pinch of salt in a bowl and mix well together.

In a jug whisk the oil, egg and milk together.

Add the wet to the dry ingredients and combine well, then add the cherries and chocolate. The mixture should be soft but not too runny or too thick.

Divide the mixture between the muffin cases and then cook for 20-25 minutes or until well risen and golden.

PLAIN SCONES

MAKES: 12
PREPARATION: 10mins
COOKING: 10-12mins

Scones are one of the hardest things to replicate gluten-free. I think I've cracked it with this recipe though!

300g gluten-free flour mix (see recipe on page 152)
4 teaspoons gluten-free baking powder
1 tablespoon caster sugar
2 teaspoons xanthan gum
100g unsalted butter
2 medium eggs
125ml milk

salt
butter, for greasing
flour, for rolling out
1 beaten egg, for glazing
strawberry jam and clotted cream, to serve

Preheat the oven to 220°C/425°F/gas mark 7. Lightly grease a baking tray.

Sift all the dry ingredients and a pinch of salt into a large bowl. Lightly rub the butter into the flour mix. Make a well in the centre of the mixture.

Beat the eggs and milk together and add to the well in the flour and butter. Mix to a soft dough.

Turn out the dough onto a floured surface; press out with the palm of your hand, to about 2cm thick, and then cut out 12 rounds using a 6cm cutter. Gently place on the baking tray and brush with a little beaten egg.

Bake until well risen and golden brown, about 10 minutes.

Remove from the oven and transfer to a wire cooling rack. Eat the scones nice and fresh, sliced and spread with jam and cream.

FUDGY ALMOND CAKE WITH MINT SYRUP AND FROSTING

A great combination of moreish ingredients here – mint, chocolate and honeycomb. Cakes and pastry are notoriously difficult to replicate with gluten-free alternatives but this one is a real winner – it's a moist, well-flavoured cake with a crunchy topping.

For the cake

200g unsalted butter

200g gluten-free dark chocolate (minimum 70 per cent cocoa solids), broken into pieces

5 medium eggs, at room temperature, separated

pinch of cream of tartar

240g caster sugar

1 tablespoon vanilla extract

200g ground almonds

50g chickpea (gram) flour

For the syrup

100g caster sugar

4 tablespoons chopped fresh mint

For the frosting

500g mascarpone

50g honeycomb, chopped

100g clear honey

Preheat the oven to 180°C/350°F/gas mark 4. Line a 24cm round, 7cm deep, loose-bottomed cake tin with baking parchment.

Place the butter and chocolate in a heatproof bowl and melt over a pan of simmering water. Once melted, take the pan off the heat but leave the bowl over the pan to keep the mixture warm.

Place the egg whites and cream of tartar in a bowl and whisk until thick and foamy, then add half the sugar, and whisk again until creamy and thick.

Add the rest of the sugar and whisk until very stiff, but still a creamy consistency. Stir the egg yolks, vanilla extract, almonds and chickpea flour into the warm chocolate and butter, then straight away add half the meringue, mixing well.

Finally, add the rest of the meringue and fold in.

Spoon into the lined tin and bake for 45-50 minutes, or until well risen and firm.

Remove from the oven and cool slightly in the tin; it will collapse a little. Make several holes over the surface of the cake with a skewer.

Meanwhile, place the sugar, 100ml water and the mint in a small pan and boil until the sugar has dissolved, then strain. Spoon the syrup over the cake and leave to soak in and cool completely.

Once the cake has cooled, beat the mascarpone, honeycomb and honey together with a wooden spoon or spatula. Do not whisk or the mascarpone will be too soft and not hold its shape on the cake.

Turn out the cake carefully onto a large, flat plate. As there is no gluten in the cake it will have quite a soft texture, so be careful. Cover the cake with the honey mascarpone.

Eat straight away or chill for 1 hour. If you want to keep it for the next day, remove from the fridge 1 hour before eating.

SQUIDGY CHESTNUT MERINGUE CAKE

SERVES: 6-8
PREPARATION: 10mins
COOKING: 1¼ hours

I developed this recipe a few years ago and have made it many times and it never fails to impress. Chestnut purée, an ingredient not often used these days, gives it a delicious flavour. Once made, the longer you leave the cake in the fridge the squidgier it becomes. It makes a great Christmas pudding alternative.

4 medium egg whites at room temperature

pinch of cream of tartar

230g caster sugar

1 teaspoon cornflour

1 teaspoon vanilla extract

1 teaspoon vinegar

600ml double cream

100g tinned unsweetened chestnut purée, broken up with a fork

200ml Irish cream liqueur

juice of ½ lemon

icing sugar, to dust

Preheat the oven to 130°C/250°F/gas mark ½. Line a 37 x 27cm Swiss roll tin with baking parchment. Place the egg whites and cream of tartar in a mixing bowl and whisk until light and foamy. Add half the sugar and whisk well until thick and glossy, but not overbeaten. If you overwhisk, the meringue will become dull and firm. Add the rest of the sugar and just bring together, say for 2 minutes. Fold in the cornflour, vanilla and vinegar and mix well.

Spread into the prepared tin and cook for 1 hour 15 minutes. Remove from the oven and cool slightly, then cut into 3 even-sized pieces. Set aside to cool completely. Place the double cream, chestnut purée and Irish cream liqueur in a mixing bowl and whisk together until fairly thick, then add the lemon juice; do not overwhisk.

Quickly spread half the cream over one of the meringues, then top with a second piece, then add the rest of the cream and finally the last layer of meringue.

Press down with a wire cooling rack (this keeps it even) and dust well with icing sugar. Place in the fridge for 1 hour to set and soften. The cake can then be chilled for up to 4 hours before serving. Slice and serve.

MAKES: 2 x 23cm round cakes
PREPARATION: 15mins
COOKING: 25-30mins

BIRTHDAY CAKE SPONGE

As a basic sponge this recipe is rather good. The glycerine helps to keep the sponge softer, as does the butter. Once cooked though it will dry out quickly, due to the rice flour reconstituting itself, so wrap it carefully in foil or eat fresh. I won't go into detail regarding the decoration; I'm sure you have your own special way!

225g unsalted butter, at room temperature

397g tin condensed milk, at room
   temperature

75g potato starch

200g brown rice flour

4 medium eggs, beaten

3 level teaspoons gluten-free baking powder

3 teaspoons vanilla extract

2 teaspoons glycerine

3 tablespoons olive oil

butter and brown rice flour, to prepare the cake tins

filling and decorations of your choice

Preheat the oven to 180°C/350°F/gas mark 4. Grease 2 x 23cm round cake tins really well, then dust with brown rice flour. Knock out the excess flour.

Place the softened butter and condensed milk in a mixing bowl and mix them together. Add the starch, rice flour and beaten eggs and stir well.

Next, add the baking powder, vanilla extract, glycerine, oil and 3 tablespoons of warm water and mix well, preferably with an electric whisk.

Spoon or pour the mixture into the prepared tins. Bake for 25-30 minutes, until well risen and lightly browned.

Once cooked, leave to cool in the tins. Once cooled, remove from the tins. To finish, sandwich together with your favourite filling and decorate as desired.

This cake is best eaten fresh, but you can wrap it in foil or clingfilm for up to 2 days until needed.

SERVES: 4-6
PREPARATION: 15mins
plus overnight freezing
COOKING: none

EASY ICED BLACKCURRANT MOUSSE

This is a good way of making a version of ice cream without an ice cream machine. It's quick and easy and has a deliciously smooth texture. I like to serve it after a big dinner or lunch – all you need is a little extra blackcurrant purée and fresh fruit to serve. Great tip here, fresh blackcurrants do not make a nice purée, but if you freeze them first, then thaw and liquidise, they transform into a beautiful, deep-coloured sauce. The same can be said for raspberries, the deeper colour and flavour is just as good as fresh purée.

450g frozen blackcurrants, thawed

4 medium egg whites, at room temperature

pinch of cream of tartar

125g caster sugar, preferably unrefined

250ml double cream, lightly whipped

vegetable oil, for greasing

fresh fruit, to serve

Oil a 900g loaf tin and line it with clingfilm. Place the thawed blackcurrants and lemon juice in a food processor or liquidiser and process until nice and thick. You will end up with roughly 350ml of purée. Pass it through a fine sieve to get rid of all the pips and skins.

Next, whisk the egg whites with the cream of tartar in a large bowl until lightly foamy but holding their own weight. Add half the sugar and beat until very firm and glossy, then add the rest of the sugar and whisk until very firm.

Fold the cream into the meringue, then add 250ml of the purée and carefully fold together. Pour the mixture into the prepared tin. Cover with clingfilm and freeze overnight.

To serve, unmould the mousse and cut it into slices, arrange on plates with the remaining purée and a little fresh fruit.

RED WINE SYLLABUB WITH RAISINS

MAKES: 4
PREPARATION: 15mins
COOKING: 5mins

I first made this when I made a film on Georgian cookery. This recipe (without the raisins) was used in Georgian times to top a trifle. It was then decorated with crystallised flowers such as violets, marigolds, primroses or roses. If you want to go the whole hog, then you can buy magnificent crystallised flowers.

2 tea bags
85g raisins
250ml red wine
175g caster sugar
600ml double cream, very lightly whipped
finely grated zest and juice of 1 large orange
finely grated zest juice of 1 large lemon

First job, boil the kettle and make a cup of black tea using both the tea bags. Remove the tea bags and discard. Place the raisins in a small bowl and pour the tea over the raisins. Leave to cool completely, then strain well.

Stir most of the red wine (set aside a little for serving) and the sugar into the whipped cream and whisk until very soft. Set aside ½ teaspoon of the orange and lemon zest for decorating, then stir the remaining zest and orange and lemon juices into the cream; the mixture will thicken.

Divide the raisins and the remaining red wine between 4 glasses, then pipe or spoon the cream mixture in. Chill well. Serve topped with the reserved zest.

SERVES: 6-8
PREPARATION: 20mins
COOKING: 35-40mins

BAKEWELL PUDDING (TART)

I've done quite a bit of research into the origins of this tart or pudding and it all seems very complicated! From what I can gather, the original Bakewell recipe has many claimants. One thing I do know is that a pudding or cake was sold in the town of Bakewell many years before the Bakewell Tart was supposedly first made. My recipe has no flour and relies on almonds and eggs to get a lovely pudding. The centre will sink considerably but that's quite normal.

For the pastry

100g cornflour

100g rice flour

80g unrefined caster sugar

100g butter, chilled and cut into small cubes

juice of 1 small lime

finely grated zest of 1 small orange

cornflour, for dusting

For the filling

3 tablespoons apricot jam

3 tablespoons seedless raspberry jam

2 medium eggs

125g caster sugar

125g unsalted butter, melted

125g ground almonds

lightly whipped cream, to serve

Preheat the oven to 180°C/350°F/gas mark 4. Place the cornflour, rice flour and sugar together in a food processor and blend well. Add the cubed butter and blitz until it resembles fine breadcrumbs. Add the lime juice and orange zest and bring together, then turn out and knead the dough.

Roll the dough out quickly and evenly, using a little extra cornflour and use to line a 24 x 3cm round non-stick, deep pie dish. Line the pastry with greaseproof paper and baking beans. Bake for 15 minutes to set and lightly colour the pastry.

Turn the oven up to 190°C/375°F/gas mark 5. Spread both the jams onto the part-cooked pastry base. Meanwhile, place the eggs and sugar in a mixing bowl and whisk until very stiff - about 15 minutes on high speed.

Pour in the melted butter and mix carefully. Next, fold in the ground almonds and spoon the mixture into the pastry shell. Bake for 20-25 minutes or until the sponge is cooked and the pastry light brown. Cool and serve with a little lightly whipped cream.

WARM MOUSSELINE GLAZED MANDARINS

I quite like tinned fruit, especially peaches and mandarins. Here is a simple pud, that can be knocked up pretty quickly from a few basic ingredients. It is especially good served with blackcurrant or raspberry sorbet. A word of warning though: make sure the egg is well cooked when whisking over the pan of boiling water or it will split when warmed under the grill.

2 x 420g tins mandarin oranges
5 medium egg yolks
100g caster sugar
100ml white wine

zest of 1 large lemon
100ml whipping cream
blackcurrant or raspberry sorbet, to serve

Open the tins of mandarins and empty into a colander to drain them well.

Place the egg yolks, caster sugar and white wine in a heatproof mixing bowl and place on the top pan of gently simmering water. Whisk until you have a thick, foamy mixture; this will take a few minutes.

Take the bowl off the pan of water, add the lemon zest and continue to whisk until the mixture is cool. By this stage it should be very thick. This process can be speeded up by placing the bowl in a larger bowl filled with half water and half ice cubes.

Arrange the well-drained mandarins in the bottom of a 24cm square ovenproof dish.

Preheat the grill to its hottest setting.

Gradually add the whipping cream to the egg mixture until you have a soft mousse texture, being careful not to add too much as the mixture spreads when it is cooked.

Pour the egg mixture over the mandarins and place the dish under the grill until the egg mixture is a nice golden brown.

Serve warm with blackcurrant or raspberry sorbet.

TOFFEE RIPPLE CHEESECAKE WITH BLUEBERRY STEW

SERVES: 6-8
PREPARATION: 30mins
plus 1 hour setting
plus overnight chilling
COOKING: 45mins

This is a New York-style cheesecake – smooth and perfectly creamy.

For the base

55g unsalted butter

1 tablespoon golden syrup

½ quantity Orange and Lime Shortbread (see page 159), cooked and broken into crumbs

25g cocoa powder

butter, for greasing

For the filling

400g cream cheese

115g caster sugar

1 tablespoon cornflour

3 medium eggs

3 tablespoons lemon juice

1½ teaspoons pure vanilla extract

400ml crème fraîche

397g tin Carnation Caramel (dulce de leche)

For the stew

500g fresh blueberries

2 tablespoons brown sugar

100ml fresh orange juice

1 level tablespoon cornflour

2 tablespoons cold water

Preheat the oven to 180°C/350°F/gas mark 4. Base-line a 20cm round springform tin with baking parchment, then grease the lined tin. To make the base, melt the butter and golden syrup in a medium pan. Blend the shortbread crumbs and cocoa powder into fine crumbs in a food processor, then combine with the butter mixture. Lightly press into the tin, making an even layer and chill well.

In a food processor, blend the cream cheese and sugar until smooth. Add the cornflour and blend again before adding the eggs, one at a time, with the processor running. Finally, add the lemon juice, vanilla and crème fraîche and blend until smooth.

Tightly wrap the base of the chilled tin in foil and then repeat with a double layer, so it's well up the side of the tin and pour the filling onto the biscuit base. Place the tin in a roasting tin. Warm the Carnation Caramel in a small pan and gently ripple it onto the filling, allowing it to fall from a spoon. Fill the roasting tin with 2.5cm of very hot water, it should not come over the foil. Bake the cheesecake in the centre of the oven for 45 minutes.

Turn off the oven and leave for 1 hour to set without opening the door. Then transfer to a wire cooling rack and chill overnight. Place the blueberries, sugar and orange juice in a saucepan and gently bring to the boil, simmering until the blueberries pop. Mix the cornflour with the cold water in a cup and add to the stew, stirring all the time. Once thickened remove from the heat straight away and cool. Serve the cheesecake well chilled, with a spoonful or two of blueberry stew over each slice.

SERVES: 4-6
PREPARATION: 10mins
plus chilling
COOKING: none

TANGY LIME MOUSSE WITH MINT MUDDLE

I love this mousse – when I made it on the Paul O'Grady show I had loads of requests for the recipe. It really is so simple and very nice to eat. Bea Harling, my friend and colleague, came up with the mint muddle. Muddling was the old name given to grinding sugar and mint together. It makes a great foil for the richness of the pudding.

397g tin condensed milk

400g cream cheese

finely grated zest and juice of large 4 limes

12 mint leaves

2 tablespoons granulated sugar

juice of 2 lemons

Place the condensed milk and cream cheese in a mixing bowl and whisk until thick and soft, about 7-8 minutes. Add the lime zest and juice and mix for 15 seconds. Spoon into ramekins, then chill well.

Using a pestle and mortar, crush the mint leaves with the sugar and lemon juice – this should take about 2 minutes.

Spoon the mint muddle over the set mousse and serve; it's as easy as that!

SERVES: 4
PREPARATION: 25mins
COOKING: 10mins

REALLY EASY CHOCOLATE MOUSSE

This is an easy fail-safe recipe that works well every time. It's been one of my favourites for the best part of 20 years – I bet it'll become one of yours too!

1 large egg

2 egg yolks

400g gluten-free dark chocolate (minimum 70 per cent cocoa solids), broken into pieces

375ml whipping cream, lightly whipped

1 tablespoon brandy

4 teaspoons boiling water

4 teaspoons instant coffee granules

4 heaped tablespoons icing sugar

220ml crème fraîche

grated chocolate (minimum 70 per cent cocoa solids), to decorate

Place the egg and yolks in a heatproof bowl over a pan of gently simmering water and whisk until thick and foamy.

Place the chocolate in a heatproof bowl over a pan of gently simmering water to melt. Remove the egg bowl from the pan, then add the melted chocolate to the hot egg froth and whisk, don't worry if it splits and looks thick. Next, add half the cream, whisking really quickly until smooth. Finally whisk in the remaining cream and the brandy. Spoon or pour into small glasses and chill.

To make the topping, mix the boiling water and coffee together, then cool slightly. Add the icing sugar and crème fraîche; mix well.

To serve, remove the glasses from the fridge and top with the coffee crème fraîche and a little grated chocolate.

BRAMLEY APPLE AND PEAR CRUMBLE

SERVES: 4-6
PREPARATION: 10mins
COOKING: 35-40mins

I first cooked this on *This Morning*, and the response was huge. It's very simple to make, and rice flour really gives a nice crunchy edge to the pudding. In fact, I prefer it to a crumble made with plain flour.

For the fruit

2 large Bramley apples, peeled, cored and
    roughly chopped
50g soft brown sugar
zest and juice of 1 large orange
1 vanilla pod, split and seeds scraped out
4 ripe pears, peeled, cored and cut into 8 pieces

For the topping

300g brown rice flour
150g unsalted butter, chilled
salt
150g caster sugar
custard or vanilla ice cream, to serve

Preheat the oven to 200°C/400°F/gas mark 6. Place the apples, sugar, orange zest and juice and vanilla seeds in a saucepan and gently heat. Cook until the apples are half cooked, but not a complete mush. Next, add the pears and warm through for a couple of minutes, to start the cooking process. Spoon the fruit into a 24 x 24 x 4cm baking dish.

Place the rice flour and butter in a food processor, add a couple of pinches of salt and blitz until smooth. Just pulse in the sugar, do not overwork.

Carefully spoon the crumble over the fruit mixture, but do not pack down.

Bake for 25-30 minutes, or until well browned and cooked.

Serve with custard or ice cream.

ROASTED PEACHES
WITH BUTTERSCOTCH

SERVES: 4
PREPARATION: 10mins
COOKING: 15mins

This dish really relies on the ripeness of the peaches; if they're not ripe, you will not be able to stone them. Most of the supermarkets now sell - wait for it...ripe fruit; call me old fashioned - isn't that the point.

Peaches and butterscotch work really well together - enjoy!

140g soft brown sugar
80g unsalted butter
300ml double cream
6 ripe peaches, halved and stoned
vanilla ice cream, to serve

Preheat the oven to 220°C/425°F/gas mark 7. Place the sugar and 40g of the butter in a small pan, heat gently and once the butter has melted bring to the boil. Add the cream and bring to the boil, stirring all the time so the sauce does not stick.

When the cream has completely melted, pass through a fine sieve and cover with clingfilm.

Heat an ovenproof frying pan, then add the remaining butter, and heat until it starts to sizzle and turn slightly brown. Add the peach halves, cut-side down, cook for 1 minute, then pop into the oven. Depending on the ripeness of the peaches cook for 3-4 minutes. They need to be warm, but not mushy.

Spoon the cooked peaches into a serving bowl, then pour over half the sauce. Serve the peaches with the extra sauce and vanilla ice cream.

SERVES: 6-8
PREPARATION: 20mins
COOKING: 1 hour

CAROLE'S NO-FLOUR ORANGE CAKE

This recipe came from my friend Polly's mum Carole; it's delicious, and quite unusual. Whole oranges are pierced (important or they may explode!) and then cooked in the microwave to give a fantastic fruity flavour to this delicious flour-free cake.

2 medium oranges
3 medium eggs
250g caster sugar
finely grated zest of 1 large lemon
200g ground almonds
50g chestnut flour

1 level teaspoon gluten-free baking powder
1 level teaspoon xanthan gum
butter, for greasing
natural yogurt, crème fraîche or whipped cream,
   to serve

Preheat the oven to 180°C/350°F/gas mark 4. Lightly grease a 20cm round loose-bottomed, non-stick cake tin.

Make several slits in the oranges, place in a heatproof bowl, cover with clingfilm, pierce and microwave on High power for 5-10 minutes until very soft and cooked. Once cooked you should be able to push a knife through without any resistance whatsoever.

Cool the oranges and then chop finely, or pulse in a food processor: take care because you don't want a purée.

Place the eggs and sugar in a bowl and whisk on a high speed for about 10 minutes or until really thick and foamy.

Gently fold the cooked oranges into the egg mixture followed by the lemon zest, almonds, chestnut flour, baking powder and xanthan gum; don't go mad with the stirring.

Pour into the greased cake tin and cook for 45 minutes, or until well coloured and slightly risen.

Once cooked, cool in the tin and then turn out. Slice and serve with a little natural yogurt, crème fraîche or whipped cream.

BAKED INDIAN RICE PUDDING WITH NUTS, FRUIT AND SAFFRON

SERVES: 4
PREPARATION: 5mins
COOKING: 1 hour

I like rice pud in any shape or form; this is a lovely twist on the classic nursery favourite and it can be enjoyed hot or cold.

410g tin evaporated milk

200ml full-fat milk

pinch of saffron threads

55g short grain rice

2 tablespoons soft brown sugar

2 tablespoons pistachios, roughly chopped

1 tablespoon roughly chopped unblanched almonds

4 cardamom pods, crushed

2 tablespoons sultanas

Preheat the oven to 180°C/350°F/gas mark 4. Pour the evaporated milk into a measuring jug. Top up with the milk until you have 600ml. Pour the milk into a flameproof heavy-based casserole dish (preferably non-stick), add the saffron and bring to the boil very slowly. Once the milk is boiling, sprinkle in the rice and stir well.

Cover with a tight-fitting lid and bake in the oven for about 1 hour, stirring every 10-15 minutes. Add brown sugar to taste and stir well. Finally, stir in the chopped nuts and sultanas. Leave for a few minutes for the sultanas to soften, then serve.

SERVES: 4
PREPARATION: 20mins
plus chilling
COOKING: none

LIGHT PINK GRAPEFRUIT MOUSSE

This beautiful tangy mousse is really so simple, and can also be made with oranges or normal grapefruit.

juice and segments of 4 pink grapefruit

50g icing sugar

6 small leaves bronze gelatine, soaked or 10g gelatine
   powder

250ml double cream

icing sugar, to dust

Line a 23cm cake tin with clingfilm. Segment all the grapefruit and squeeze the remaining membranes and flesh into a measuring jug and make up to 300ml with cold water.

Meanwhile warm half the grapefruit juice in a small pan and add the icing sugar. Dissolve the soaked or powdered gelatine in the juice and sugar.

Add the two juices together and then stir in the double cream.

Finally, stir in half the segments and reserve the remainder for decoration. The mixture should hold its own weight; if not, chill slightly until it starts to thicken.

Spoon into the lined cake tin or mould and chill well.

Top with the remaining grapefruit segments in a neat pattern and dust with icing sugar. Turn out of the tin, slice and serve.

OVEN-POACHED RHUBARB WITH MOUSSELINE SAUCE

SERVES: 6
PREPARATION: 15mins plus chilling
COOKING: 40mins

As I have said many times before, less is more; well this is certainly the rule with this pud. Nice and easy, but really tasty to eat.

For the rhubarb
350g new season rhubarb, cut into 10cm lengths
150g caster sugar
2 vanilla pods, split and seeds scraped out
juice of 1 large lime

For the sauce
6 egg yolks
100g caster sugar
100ml medium white wine
zest of 1 fresh lime plus a squeeze of juice
100ml double cream, very lightly whipped

Preheat the oven to 180°C/350°F/gas mark 4. Lay the rhubarb into a 25cm square 3cm deep baking dish. Sprinkle over the caster sugar, vanilla seeds, lime juice and 4 tablespoons of cold water, then cover with foil. Bake in the oven for 35-40 minutes or until the rhubarb is soft but still whole. Remove from the oven and cool. Cover with clingfilm and chill.

To make the sauce, place the egg yolks, caster sugar and white wine in a heatproof bowl. Whisk quickly over a pan of gently simmering water until the eggs thicken and cook.

Take care not to let the eggs scramble – the secret is to keep removing the bowl from the pan, keep whisking and replacing onto the pan, so the egg yolks cook evenly. When cooked they will be thick and foamy.

Remove from the pan and continue to whisk until cold and very thick. Stir in the lime zest and juice and double cream.

To serve, take the rhubarb out of the fridge and remove the clingfilm. Then pour over the sauce and serve straight away.

CONVERSION CHART

WEIGHT (SOLIDS)	
7g	¼oz
10g	½oz
20g	¾oz
25g	1oz
40g	1½oz
50g	2oz
60g	2½oz
75g	3oz
100g	3½oz
110g	4oz (¼lb)
125g	4½oz
150g	5½oz
175g	6oz
200g	7oz
225g	8oz (½lb)
250g	9oz
275g	10oz
300g	10½oz
310g	11oz
325g	11½oz
350g	12oz (¾lb)
375g	13oz
400g	14oz
425g	15oz
450g	1lb
500g (½kg)	18oz
600g	1¼lb
700g	1½lb
750g	1lb 10oz
900g	2lb
1kg	2¼lb
1.1kg	2½lb
1.2kg	2lb 12oz
1.3kg	3lb
1.5kg	3lb 5oz
1.6kg	3½lb
1.8kg	4lb
2kg	4lb 8oz
2.25kg	5lb
2.5kg	5lb 8oz
3kg	6lb 8oz

VOLUME (LIQUIDS)	
5ml	1 teaspoon
10ml	1 dessertspoon
15ml	1 tablespoon or ½fl oz
30ml	1fl oz
40ml	1½fl oz
50ml	2fl oz
60ml	2½fl oz
75ml	3fl oz
100ml	3½fl oz
125ml	4fl oz
150ml	5fl oz (¼ pint)
160ml	5½fl oz
175ml	6fl oz
200ml	7fl oz
225ml	8fl oz
250ml (0.25 litre)	9fl oz
300ml	10fl oz (½ pint)
325ml	11fl oz
350ml	12fl oz
370ml	13fl oz
400ml	14fl oz
425ml	15fl oz (¾ pint)
450ml	16fl oz
500ml (0.5 litre)	18fl oz
550ml	19fl oz
600ml	20fl oz (1 pint)
700ml	1¼ pints
850ml	1½ pints
1 litre	1¾ pints
1.2 litres	2 pints
1.5 litres	2½ pints
1.8 litres	3 pints
2 litres	3½ pints

LENGTH	
5mm	¼ inch
1cm	½ inch
2cm	¾ inch
2.5cm	1 inch
3cm	1¼ inches
4cm	1½ inches
5cm	2 inches
7.5 cm	3 inches
10cm	4 inches
15cm	6 inches
18cm	7 inches
20cm	8 inches
24cm	10 inches
28cm	11 inches
30cm	12 inches

INDEX

ACKNOWLEDGEMENTS

Well, where do I start? This book has been by far the most difficult I have written, due to the precise nature of the recipes and the background to them all.

Fern, what can I say? Thank you for all the support and help; what a lucky bloke I am...

Norma McGough, Amy Peterson, Emma Merrikin, Kathryn Miller, Kate Newman from Coeliac UK have been an incredible help, not only in getting this whole project off the ground, but for helping out in so many ways whilst I was cooking and writing.

Danielle Di Michiel and Kyle, for putting faith in the original idea, thank you.

John Rush and Luigi Bonomi, great agents and friends.

Clare Greenstreet, the home economist and Bea Harling, for testing all the recipes I struggled with and for her brilliant knowledge of food science. Long-suffering Julia Alger, for shopping, cooking and editing my scribble, brilliant job as always. Steve Poole and Tim Sutcliffe, who worked incredibly hard setting up the original puddings idea. Steve Lee, for really going the extra mile with a bad back – the best food photographer around. Thanks to you all.